United Synagogue of Conservative Judaism • Department of Youth Activities

WHO RENEWS CREATION

Earl Schwartz

Barry D. Cytron

מְחַדֵּשׁ בְּכָל יוֹם תָּמִיד מַעֲשֵׂה בְרֵאשִׁית

UNITED SYNAGOGUE OF CONSERVATIVE JUDAISM
DEPARTMENT OF YOUTH ACTIVITIES

Jules A. Gutin, *Director*
Gila R. Hadani, *Program Director*
Ari Y. Goldberg, *Education Director*
Stuart Friedman, *Projects Coordinator*
Robert Gamer, *Activities Coordinator*
Shira Plain, *Outreach Coordinator*
Jonathan Hammer-Kossoy, *Publications Coordinator*
Shalom Orzach, *Central Shaliach*
Yitzchak Jacobsen, *Director, Israel Office*
David Keren, *Nativ Director*

NATIONAL YOUTH COMMISSION

Marshall P. Baltuch, *Chairman*

UNITED SYNAGOGUE OF CONSERVATIVE JUDAISM

Alan Ades, *President*
Rabbi Jerome M. Epstein, *Executive Vice President*

A publication of the National Youth Commission,
United Synagogue of Conservative Judaism,
155 Fifth Avenue, New York, New York 10010
Second Edition, 1995

Manufactured in the United States of America
Cover design by Graphics Workshop

Library of Congress Catalog Card Number: 93-061536

Photographs courtesy of the Jewish Historical Society of the Upper Midwest

Printed on Recycled Paper

Dedication

For Rabbi Mosheh B. Sachs

and

Rabbi Bernard Lipnick

Acknowledgements

Writing a book of this sort is like running a relay race. As its authors, we ran only a portion of that race, in as much as each time we finished a piece of the manuscript, others were waiting to help carry it to completion. We deeply appreciate the generous and thoughtful assistance we have received from all our "running partners."

We would especially like to thank Jacob Blumenthal, who managed the project and authored many of Mrs. Saltz's and Yoni's "marginal comments," as well as the group activities. It was a pleasure working with such a patient, receptive, and hardworking "*ba'al ha-bayit.*"

We would also like to thank our manuscript readers: Rabbi Jerome M. Epstein, Ari Goldberg, Jonathan S. Greenberg, Jules Gutin, Rabbi Eliot Marrus, Rabbi Lawrence Troster, Amy Wasser, and Rabbi Joel Wasser. Their careful reading of early versions of the book provided us with valuable suggestions for improving the final text. We also appreciate the guidance provided by Rabbis Everett Gendler and Steven Shaw.

Special thanks to Ari Goldberg, who helped to coordinate our efforts, to Warren Patterson for showing us how to attach a tractor to a thresher, and to Max Goodman, for reminding us that all good ideas come "b'ezrat ha-Shem."

Finally, we would like to thank Rabbis Bernard Lipnick and Moshe Sachs, our models for the wise and worldly Rabbi Gordon. As a token of our respect for their dedication to a vision of the world made better through Torah, we dedicate this book to them.

E.S. & B.D.C.

Table of Contents

Foreword

Sir Thomas More gave us the term **Utopia**, which actually means "no-place." More was speaking of a place where human beings could live happy and just lives, in a society that cultivated the best in the individual for the welfare of all.

More lived in early sixteenth century England, when Europeans first received news of lands on the far side of the Atlantic. His book *Utopia* was strongly influenced by the excitement and wonder these reports engendered. He placed his "utopia" in what Europeans would come to call the "Americas," though the title *Utopia* was intended to indicate his own doubts about human beings ever finding, or founding, such a place.

More was, however, not the first to conceive of a "utopia." Two thousand years earlier, the famous Greek philosopher Plato conceived of a similar place he called the "Republic." Plato built his ideal republic with what he believed were the very best social, economic and political materials of his day, including elements of both Spartan and Athenian society.

If a group of Jews were to set sail for Utopia, what map would they follow, and what materials would they bring with them? Would a Jewish utopia resemble More's or Plato's? What would be their blueprint for building an authentic Jewish utopia?

These are not idle questions. During the past century, many Jews have sought to find their own type of utopia, where they could live happy and just lives. For some, that meant heading for Palestine, now Israel, inspired by Zionist thinkers like Theodor Herzl and A. D. Gordon. Other Jews sought fulfillment of their dream in the Americas. To be sure, some who came to these shores were content just to make a living and take care of their family. Others, however, dreamed that they could create ways of life that were far, far better than those they had left behind. The most daring among them actually took upon themselves the challenge of living out their fondest hopes by founding ideal communities of their own design.

This sourcebook tells the story of one such group of Jews, those who faced the challenging task of building their own sort of utopia, a true Jewish community on the North Dakota prairie at the beginning of this century. We have been inspired to create their story based on the actual experience of Jewish farmers of North

1

Dakota who sought to build a new life and a new type of community here in the Americas.

The questions we have asked are: **What challenges would be faced by Jews intent on creating not simply an efficient and prosperous community, but a Jewish one, based on the central norms and highest ideals of rabbinic Judaism? How would they incorporate those teachings into the structure of a living community? More specifically, what could the Torah teach those farmers about the land they lived on, and how they should treat it, its water and other resources, and the creatures that inhabited that world with them?**

Part I of this sourcebook tells the story of how this Jewish community might have faced such a challenge. Part II brings their story into our own day. In many ways, the environmental issues raised in Part I -- from using the land, to caring for wildlife, to respecting the rights of neighbors -- are much more problematic today than could ever have been anticipated before. The principles and norms that might have sufficed to answer the concerns of North Dakota farmers at the beginning of this century must be reshaped and rethought for our largely urban communities at the end of this century. In Part II, we invite you to ponder how those earlier rabbinic teachings can continue to inform the choices we make about how we treat our environment and all that lives within it.

Both parts of the sourcebook have been cast in the form of **Sh'aylot u'Teshuvot -- Questions and Responses**. Throughout the ages, both individual Jews, and even entire communities, have sought out the advice of rabbis. Frequently, that has required seeking advice from rabbinic authorities in distant locales. These inquiries have sparked important, sometimes ground breaking, answers by the rabbis consulted. Out of respect to this richly important literature of our tradition, we have imagined what sort of questions might have been asked by a group of North Dakota Jewish farmers to a rabbi of their generation, as well as what sort of responses might be forthcoming today from a contemporary rabbi seeking to help make the letters containing those *sh'aylot* more meaningful.

Sir Thomas More called his thoroughly good land "no-place" because he believed that human beings were not equal to the challenges of living in a utopian society. But this doubt did not deter him from *imagining* the challenges. Envisioning a *best* world can often light the way to a *better* world.

Jews do this through the study of Torah and the other great sources that flow from it. Each *mitzvah* we do, no matter how homely or limited it may seem, carries within it a spark from a better world that could come to be. All great and enduring human endeavors come to fruition as the result of untold daily approximations of ideals that remain, by themselves, unattainable.

This sourcebook is about a group of Jews who take upon themselves the challenge of building the kind of community the Torah envisions for us. We hope that many Jews today still aspire to be part of such a community. Thus, we believe that the questions those North Dakota Jews ask, they ask for us all. As Rabbi Tarfon says in the *Pirkei Avot* [Ethics of the Sages]: "The day is already waning, and there is still much left to do...."

E.S. & B.D.C.
St. Paul, MN.
Heshvan 3, 5754

GROUP ACTIVITY

- **In the space below, describe your vision of a utopian society. Where would it be located? Which Jewish values would guide you?**

_____

_____

_____

_____

_____

_____

_____

- **What elements of the utopia you have described above relate to the physical environment? Why was this important, or unimportant, to you?**

- **Did you envision an agrarian society? An industrial society? A "spiritual" society? Why do you think you made such a choice?**

Chapter I: Introduction

Finding Some Letters

My name is Yoni. One Sunday morning in January, 1991, while rummaging through a box of family mementos and photos, I happened to come across a thick packet of yellowed paper. Tied to the top of the bundle were two photos. They were heavy, old-fashioned prints, well worn at the corners. I eased them out of the binder and found that they were both photos of a middle-aged couple. In one, the couple stood on a road that stretched on to the horizon behind them, with some sort of grain or prairie grass growing on either side. In the other, the two of them were standing in front of a large, barn-like building. I slipped the pictures back into the bundle and turned the sheath of papers over. Handwritten lines in dark ink had seeped through the paper, re-emerging in a blur on the outside. Though I thought I knew what I'd find in the box, I had never noticed these particular photos and papers before.

My parents were in the living room, sharing the couch and the Sunday paper. I placed the bundle in front of them and said, "Do you know who these people are?" Both of them took a long look before indicating that they didn't know anything about the pictures. "What are these papers?" my mother asked, as she carefully peeled back the first sheet. As the other side of the page came into view, we realized that it was filled with Hebrew letters, but as they stretched on across the page I found that I couldn't recognize a single word.

Meanwhile, my father was taking a closer look at the photos. On the back of one of them (I think it was the barn picture), he found what appeared to be a date: 1906. Here too there were Hebrew letters. These we slowly deciphered as the names "Avraham and Hannah Tevelmann," along with the words "Bismarck, North Dakota."

By now, my mother had completely separated the outermost sheet of paper from the rest of the bundle. It was clearly a letter. I realized that I hadn't recognized any Hebrew words because the letter was written in Yiddish. Here and there along the edges of the page someone with a different handwriting and in a slightly lighter ink had jotted down several comments. The letter was signed by none other than "Avraham and Hannah Tevelmann." But it was the name at the top of the page that held our attention: "*Kavod HaRav, Moreinu El̲ḥanan Halevy Schein*" [our honored rabbi, our teacher, Halevy Schein].

Elhanan Halevy Schein had come to the United States from Lithuania in 1889. By the time he left Lithuania he had become one of the most advanced of the younger students in his Yeshivah, but when he arrived in Chicago the only work he could find was as a laborer in the stockyards. At the age of 21, Schein married Esther Malkah Gold. Esther's father was a member of a small synagogue just off Devon Avenue When the rabbi of the synagogue left for a more prestigious position on the South Side, Esther's father campaigned for Elhanan's appointment as rabbi of the congregation. As you might expect, the synagogue's board of trustees was reluctant to choose a stockyard worker as their rabbi, but agreed to interview the man. As you may also have guessed, Elhanan so impressed the board with his scholarship, bearing and insights into the opportunities and challenges of American life that he was chosen as rabbi.

By 1906, Elhanan Halevy Schein had risen to prominence throughout the Midwest as a rabbi of extraordinary intelligence and sensitivity. And yet, despite his prominence, he remained faithful to his first American friends in the stockyards. Each *Erev Shabbat*, Schein would make his way down to the yards to speak with them. In this way he continued to stay informed of the specific difficulties faced by some of the poorest of Chicago's workers. Schein would offer what he could in assistance and advice, and then make his way back home to prepare for *Shabbat*. Some of the workers in the yards remembered that, as he walked through the maze of fences where the cattle were held, his lips moved in time to an unheard conversation. Some said he was singing the first Psalms of the evening service, lest he be late in arriving at the synagogue. Others thought that he was reviewing the questions and requests he had just received from the workers in the yards. But one old man used to say that it sounded to him like the rabbi was talking to the cattle.

Elhanan and Esther's third daughter, Raisel, was the mother of Jenny Freedman, and Jenny Freedman was my grandmother. Rabbi Schein's story had been passed down through the family, but until my parents and I read his name at the top of the letter, we thought that the only inheritance he left us was his good name and the short story of his life that I've just related.

For the next several minutes my mother and I carefully pried apart the remaining pages. When we had finished, seven letters, all written in Yiddish, lay before us. The sweet, musty smell of old paper hovered over them. As I stared at the neatly written lines that filled each page, I grew more and more curious about what they might reveal concerning my fabled great-great grandfather, but neither my parents nor I understood much Yiddish. Which brings us to Mrs. Saltz.

Mrs. Saltz was well known in our community as a lover of Yiddish, who took every opportunity -- community events, wedding receptions, accidental encounters in supermarket parking lots -- to recite a beloved Yiddish poem by Morris Rosenfeld or Nellie Sacks. She lived alone, surrounded by her books and her memories, in a little white house about a mile and a half south of where we lived.

Mrs. Saltz was clearly delighted by my call. She urged me to bring the letters over right away, and so about fifteen minutes later I carefully unwrapped the bundle for a second time for Mrs. Saltz. After having glanced at several pages, she declared that it would be no problem to translate the letters, and that she would call me as soon as she had completed one or two of them. I suppose there were two reasons for wanting to show me what she had translated piece by piece rather than all at once. First, she was very proud of her knowledge of Yiddish, and I'm sure she didn't mind being complimented on her work more than once. In addition, each finished letter meant another visit, which in turn always meant some time to talk, something to eat, and a little poetry.

I got a call from Mrs. Saltz right after supper on Monday evening. She had finished translating two of the letters and was wondering when I might come over to pick them up. "You're lucky you have me to do your translating," she added. "Not everyone knows how to translate a rabbi's correspondence. When you come you'll see what I mean." I told her that I'd be there in fifteen minutes.

Letter #1, translated by Mrs. Ida Saltz

18th Sh'vat, 5664

Honored Rabbi, Our Teacher, Elhanan Halevy Schein,

We are members of a small community, settled together on several adjacent farms near the town of Bismarck, North Dakota. We have been brought here from the Ukraine by a certain charitable organization, rescued from the terror of the pogroms and crushing poverty sweeping over our people there. But now we are free men and women in America, and we are intent upon creating a community that will find favor in the sight of God and our fellow human beings.

We have been settled on farmland and are preparing to plant our first crop. However, not a single one of us has ever farmed before. We were all townspeople in the Ukraine. We are bewildered by this new way of life. Many questions present themselves to us. The truth is that some of us are tempted to run away from here and become townspeople once again in Minneapolis or Chicago. But others among us say that the Torah teaches that it is good for Jews to be farmers, to grow their own food and to live close to the land. But if this is true, we will need help in creating the kind of community the *halachah* requires of us.

We will need to know more about what the Torah teaches concerning the growing of crops and raising of cattle, the sabbatical year, the sharing of scarce resources and many other matters. You must forgive our ignorance if I add that there are some among us who insist that the Torah has nothing to teach us about such things. The more learned among us know enough to reply that the holy Torah and teachings of our rabbis certainly have much light to shed on the predicaments we face, but we know too little to support this conviction.

Though we are hundreds of miles from Chicago, we have heard of your great learning, wisdom and love of our people, and so our community has delegated us, Avraham and Hannah Tevelmann, secretaries of the community, to contact you. Could you please help us in our search for the life the holy Torah intends for us? We would be deeply grateful for whatever guidance you could offer.

With heartfelt wishes for light, joy, gladness and honor for you and all Israel, we await your response.

A. and H. Tevelmann

* * * *

Letter apparently sent to A. and H. Tevelmann by HaRav Schein

26 Sh'vat, 5664

My Dear Friends, Brothers and Sisters in the Covenant of Israel,

Shalom.

I received your letter this morning. Though I have moved from task to task throughout the day, your words have not been far from my thoughts.

I would be happy to share with you what little learning I have. You have raised many difficult questions, but be assured that the wisdom of Torah covers all of human experience as the waters cover the sea. This does not mean that I will find a ready answer for every question you may ask, but I believe, as it says in the Psalms, that "God is close to all who call out, all who honestly call out," for help.

First of all, you should know that the Torah teaches that this world is God's creation. By this I mean that the world was created and continues to exist as a result of God's will and design. A thousand years ago our teacher Bachya ibn P'kudah, z"l, in his work, _Hovot Ha'Livavot_, told the following parable concerning the logic and order of Creation:

"Some people have claimed that the world came into being by accident without a Creator who originated it nor Designer to form it...But don't you see that if one were to suddenly spill some ink on a clean sheet of paper, it would be impossible that it would form orderly and legible lines of writing, as with a pen. And if one person were to show another some orderly writing that could not have been accomplished except by means of a pen, and that person were to claim that ink had spilled on the paper and that shapes of letters had formed on it of themselves, we would quickly disprove the contention, for there is no alternative but to assume that it had come about as a result of intentional design."

Rabbi Bahya's point is that the orderliness of the world reveals as clear and logical a message concerning its Author as does this very letter to you -- _l'havdil!_ -- if we but learn to read God's handwriting in creation.

9

I fear that those who see this world as a "machine without a master" will be tempted to use all the good things of the world without care or limit. Some may refer to the ways and wonders of the world as "nature," but I believe that only the word "creation" does the world justice, because it alone points to the wisdom and providence of the Creator.

The *Tanach* is filled with praise of creation. Psalm 104, in particular, sings of the wonders of the world:

God made the moon to signal special occasions, the sun knows its path to dusk.

You stretch out the darkness and it becomes night, when the creatures of the forest creep about.

Young lions roar for their prey; they seek their food from God.

Then the sun rises and they gather once again, crouching in their dens.

Then human beings go out to their labors, working until evening.

How great are your works, ha-Shem! You've made them all so wisely; the Earth is filled with your creations."

The *siddur* also calls upon us to offer praise to God for the "wonders that are with us daily," and God's renewal of Creation each day. Indeed, the Torah tells us that Yits<u>h</u>ak our father went out into the fields to pray, as did the Baal Shem Tov and his grandson, Rabbi Na<u>h</u>man of Bratslav. Listen to Rabbi Na<u>h</u>man's words:

Master of the Universe, grant me the ability to be alone; may it be my custom to go outdoors each day, among the trees and grass, among all growing

*things, and there may I be alone, and enter into
prayer, to talk with the One I belong to.*

*May I express there everything in my heart, and
may all the foliage of the field (all grasses, trees and
plants), may they all awake at my coming, to send
the power of their life into the words of my prayer,
so that my prayer and speech are made whole,
through the life and spirit of growing things, which
are made as one by their transcendent Source. May
they all be gathered into my prayer, and thus may I
be worthy to open my heart fully, in prayer,
supplication and holy speech....*

And so, my friends, it is my humble opinion that
the Torah does indeed encourage us to keep the
wonders of creation before us always. As we learn
in the Book of Genesis, we are called "Adam"
because we were drawn from the "adamah" -- the
ground. So let each of us draw close to God's
creation, wherever we may be.

I stand at your service. May God give you strength,
good health and success in all your endeavors.

Biv'rachah,

Elhanan Halevy Schein

* * * *

I stood on the bridge for half an hour or so as the last of the evening's commuters
streamed home on the highway beneath me. The bridge trembled each time a
"semi" blew past. The gathering darkness made it difficult for me to focus on any
particular car or truck. For the most part, I saw white lights coming toward me
and red lights moving away; but every once in a while I also caught the smell of
something going by. Of course the smell of car and truck exhaust was constant,
but a couple of times I also smelled a cattle truck.

Though the peak of rush hour traffic had already passed, the noise from the
highway would have drowned out most any conversation on the bridge - if there
had been anyone there for me to talk to. But I was alone, conversing with myself.

Yiddish speaking farmers in North Dakota, asking a rabbi for advice on where to live and how to treat the environment. If there hadn't been photos of the Tevelmanns I never could have imagined them, standing there on that dirt road. No "semis" booming by. No daily commute for the Tevelmanns.

And HaRav Schein's reply -- the only copy of a reply included in the bundle. What difference did it make to him, in the middle of Chicago, whether the Tevelmanns thought of the world as a "creation" or "nature?" And the stuff about the spilled ink was clever, but what help was it going to be to the Tevelmanns and their friends?

I had made it as far as the bridge on my way home from Mrs. Saltz's house before stopping to mull the whole thing over. We lived about a third of a mile from the bridge, on a street called "Oak Grove Terrace." Once, while waiting for the school bus on the corner of Oak Grove Terrace and Oak Lane - I must have been about ten or eleven at the time - it occurred to me that there probably wasn't a single oak in the whole neighborhood. I wondered if there really had been oaks in the area once upon a time, or if the names of the streets were just made up to sound woodsy. Now, as I stood on the bridge, I wondered if the oaks that may or may not have once surrounded where I stood were "nature" or "creation."

A patter of fine rain had begun to fall on the brown envelope Mrs. Saltz had given me for the letters. I quickly slid the envelope inside my jacket and trotted off toward home. In the rain and darkness I wouldn't have seen the oaks, even if they had still been there.

It took Mrs. Saltz about a week to finish translating the first two Tevelmann letters. We both concluded that the comments around the edges of the letters had been written by Rabbi Schein as outlines for his replies which, with the exception of his first letter, were not included in the bundle. Mrs. Saltz would call me every three or four days to tell me how she was doing, and sometimes I would stop by myself.

Each visit included a bite to eat, a Yiddish lesson, and a discussion of the contents of the most recent letter. By the third or fourth of these get-togethers, it began to dawn on me just how amazing the woman was. Not only was she a whiz in Yiddish, but she seemed very familiar with all the sources Rabbi Schein mentioned in his notes. Without my even asking, she took upon herself the task of tracking down and translating these sources as well. She told me that each week, when her daughter-in-law came by to help her with her shopping, they stopped at the synagogue library to pick up the books mentioned by Rabbi Schein. If she couldn't find a book in the library, she would move on to the rabbi's office. The Rabbi lent her whatever texts he had from his personal library. After that I don't know what she did. She probably had the rest of them memorized, along with the poetry. As you'll see, Mrs. Saltz and I jotted down many comments and questions on our own as we made our way through these sources.

I suppose the challenge of doing the research and the translations helped to relieve the loneliness and boredom Mrs. Saltz, no doubt, otherwise endured. She told me that she was doing the work "for the fun of it." Fun or not, I was continually amazed by how much she knew, and how much knowledge and experience she carried with her. More than once I wondered, "What will become of it all when she's gone?" So many of us live our lives trapped between the shores of a single generation. How much of a story can you write on a single line? Mrs. Saltz was different. Her learning was her ticket to a hundred generations that had preceded her, and, I suppose, her interest in me and my letters was her ticket to at least one more.

GROUP ACTIVITY

- **Ask your parents or grandparents if you have any relatives who are, or were, farmers. Are they alive today? If not, how long ago did they live? Do you think these settlers wanted to be farmers? If so, why do you think they did?**

Chapter II: Sh'aylah #1

**How much land may we cultivate?
Must we leave some untilled?**

28 Adar, 5664

Honored Rabbi, Our Teacher, Rabbi Schein,

We read your letter, dated the 26th of Sh'vat, with great joy. The bitterly cold winds that have buffeted us in this wilderness for many weeks now were turned back by your warm words.

We are encouraged by your counsel that we try to stay in this place, working the soil and living close to the land. Immediately after *Pesah*, we intend, God willing, to plant our first crop of wheat. As we write this letter, the fields around us remain a wild tangle of brown and gray, but we have been reassured by our gentile neighbors that it will indeed soon be spring. Now that the snow has begun to melt we have started the work of clearing the fields. As soon as the ground is soft we will begin to plow and plant.

The approach of the planting season, however, has led to a disagreement among us. The problem is this: Our farms are located on what seems to be an endless stretch of prairie, broken only by an occasional hill, a patch of woods, or a tree-lined stream. Given our dire poverty, you can well imagine the pressure upon us to cultivate as much of this land as possible. The birth of eight children over the winter, and the expected births of several more in the coming months (may they be born at auspicious times), means that we now have even more mouths to feed. Under these conditions, our survival depends on our bringing in a very large crop. We do not yet know what natural (or should we say "creational") disasters may beset us in the course of the coming growing season, and our ignorance of

15

the art of farming can only make the process of raising an ample crop that much more difficult. But we have no choice. Either we bring in a large crop or we will "quickly be uprooted from the good land that God has given us."

Nevertheless, a question has been posed by a member of our community named Boroch. He has urged us to reconsider simply cultivating all the land our plows can reach. Boroch points out that when one looks closely at this land, one sees that a homely clump of trees is also the home of a thousand creatures, large and small, that will certainly perish if their habitats are destroyed. This fellow claims that once destroyed, or even tampered with, these wild spaces can never be restored, and so he insists that, far from cultivating as much land as we can, we should cultivate only as much as is necessary, even if we suffer economic **Deut. 20:19-20** losses as a result. He has told us of articles he has read in English newspapers about President Roosevelt's great interest in the preservation of wildernesses, but many of us are skeptical of this last claim, in as much as we have seem many photographs of the President hunting wild animals, in America and elsewhere.

At any rate, most of us believe that all this is just **B'reisheet** plain foolishness, foolishness that we can ill-afford. **Rabbah 10:5** Our livelihood depends on our effective use of the land beneath our feet. Did God not give the Earth to human beings first of all, along with the blessing **Lev. 25:1-34** that we "Be fruitful and multiply, filling the Earth and subduing it, ruling over the fish in the sea and the birds in the sky, and over all the creatures that **Hirsch on Lev. 25:34** prowl the Earth?" (Genesis 1:28)

Most of our community is in favor of plowing as much land as possible, and in such matters we generally follow the will of the majority. Nonetheless, there is something about our comrade's argument, as foolish as it seems, that gives many of us pause. And so, the community has asked that we write to you once again for your good counsel.

What does the Torah teach us about these questions? It seems to most of us that the Torah teaches that human beings have the right to use as much land as they need. The Earth is so large. How can the cultivating of a little land to feed our hungry families be wrong? Does the Torah place any value on leaving land untouched by human activity?

Kohelet Rabbah 7

Forgive us for imposing upon you. We are aware of your busy schedule and the great responsibilities you bear, but we have nowhere else to turn. We are now, as mentioned above, beginning to prepare our fields for planting. Please respond quickly. We are, as always, deeply indebted to you for your help.

A. and H. Tevelmann

TEXTS CITED

Texts cited by Rabbi Schein in response to the question: "Does the Torah place any value on leaving land untouched by human activity?"

Deuteronomy 20:19

דברים כ : י"ט

When you lay siege to a city for a long time, battling against it to capture it, you may not destroy its trees by wielding an ax against them, because you eat of their fruit, and therefore must not cut them down; for are the trees of the field like human beings, able to flee from you as you lay siege? You may only destroy it or cut down those trees that you know are not fruit bearing trees. You may use them for laying siege to the city that is making war with you, until it is captured.

כִּי תָצוּר אֶל עִיר יָמִים רַבִּים לְהִלָּחֵם עָלֶיהָ לְתׇפְשָׂהּ לֹא תַשְׁחִית אֶת עֵצָהּ לִנְדֹּחַ עָלָיו גַּרְזֶן כִּי מִמֶּנּוּ תֹאכֵל וְאֹתוֹ לֹא תִכְרֹת כִּי הָאָדָם עֵץ הַשָּׂדֶה לָבֹא מִפָּנֶיךָ בַּמָּצוֹר. רַק עֵץ אֲשֶׁר תֵּדַע כִּי לֹא עֵץ מַאֲכָל הוּא אֹתוֹ תַשְׁחִית וְכָרָתָּ וּבָנִיתָ מָצוֹר עַל הָעִיר אֲשֶׁר הִוא עֹשָׂה עִמְּךָ מִלְחָמָה עַד רִדְתָּהּ.

17

- **This is the Biblical source for the rabbinic prohibition "against wasteful destruction" [*bal tash'hit*] of useful things. But if this is the only place in the Torah where the issue of destroying natural things is raised, the *mitzvah* of *bal tash'hit* must not have been high on the Torah's list of priorities. Or could it be that the point of this passage is that even in the extreme emergency of war, one must not thoughtlessly destroy anything; how much more so under less extreme circumstances?**

* * * *

From **B'reisheet Rabbah,** a collection of midrashim from the period of the Mishnah and Talmud. The following comment is associated in the text with the verse, "Thus the Heavens and the Earth were completed with all their array" (Gen. 2:1)

Our teachers have taught us that even those things that appear to be unnecessary additions to this world, like flies and fleas and gnats, are an integral part of creation. All things are agents of God's will. Even snakes. Even frogs!

רבנן אמרי אפיי׳ דברים שאתה רואה אותן שהן יתירה בעולם כגון זבובין ופרעושין ויתושין אף הן בכלל ברייתו של עולם הן. ובכל הלדוש ברוך הוא עושה שליחותו. אפיי עייי יתוש. אפיי עייי צפרדע.

- **Does this mean that all species have an integral role to play in the world, or that each individual creature plays such a role?**

- **If this comment refers to species, it would indicate that human beings are relatively free to act on the environment, as long as species, as a whole, are protected. What might be the consequences of maintaining such a standard?**

- **On the other hand, if the comment refers to individual creatures, it would mean that one would have to account for the impact of one's actions on the well-being of every single creature. How might such a requirement affect the way one lived one's life? What if one kills an ant? A roach? A spider? What effects might it have on the environment?**

* * * *

Leviticus 25:1-24, concerning observance of the sabbatical year:

God spoke to Moses on Mount Sinai: Speak to the Israelite people and say

וַיְדַבֵּר יְהֹוָה אֶל מֹשֶׁה בְּהַר סִינַי לֵימֹר. דַּבֵּר אֶל בְּנֵי יִשְׂרָאֵל וְאָמַרְתָּ אֲלֵהֶם כִּי תָבֹאוּ אֶל

to them: *when you enter the land that I give you, the land shall observe a Shabbat of God. Six years you may sow your field and six years you may prune your vineyard and gather in the yield. But in the seventh year the land shall have a Shabbat of complete rest, a Shabbat of God; you shall not sow your field or prune your vineyard. You shall not reap the aftergrowth of your harvest or gather the grapes of your untrimmed vines; it shall be a year of complete rest for the land. But you may eat whatever the land during its Shabbat will produce -- you, your male and female slaves, the hired and bound laborers who live with you, and your cattle and the beasts in your land may eat all its yield...And should you ask, "What are we to eat in the seventh year, if we may neither sow nor gather in our crops?" I will ordain my blessing for you in the sixth year, so that it shall yield a crop sufficient for three years...But there can be no permanent sale of land, for the land is Mine; you are but strangers residing with Me.*

הָאָרֶץ אֲשֶׁר אֲנִי נֹתֵן לָכֶם וְשָׁבְתָה הָאָרֶץ שַׁבָּת לַיהוָה. שֵׁשׁ שָׁנִים תִּזְרַע שָׂדֶךָ וְשֵׁשׁ שָׁנִים תִּזְמֹר כַּרְמֶךָ וְאָסַפְתָּ אֶת תְּבוּאָתָהּ. וּבַשָּׁנָה הַשְּׁבִיעִת שַׁבַּת שַׁבָּתוֹן יִהְיֶה לָאָרֶץ שַׁבָּת לַיהוָה שָׂדְךָ לֹא תִזְרָע וְכַרְמְךָ לֹא תִזְמֹר. אֵת סְפִיחַ קְצִירְךָ לֹא תִקְצוֹר וְאֶת עִנְּבֵי נְזִירֶךָ לֹא תִבְצֹר שְׁנַת שַׁבָּתוֹן יִהְיֶה לָאָרֶץ. וְהָיְתָה שַׁבַּת הָאָרֶץ לָכֶם לְאָכְלָה לְךָ וּלְעַבְדְּךָ וְלַאֲמָתֶךָ וְלִשְׂכִירְךָ וּלְתוֹשָׁבְךָ הַגָּרִים עִמָּךְ. וְלִבְהֶמְתְּךָ וְלַחַיָּה אֲשֶׁר בְּאַרְצֶךָ תִּהְיֶה כָל תְּבוּאָתָהּ לֶאֱכֹל.

וְכִי תֹאמְרוּ מַה נֹּאכַל בַּשָּׁנָה הַשְּׁבִיעִת הֵן לֹא נִזְרָע וְלֹא נֶאֱסֹף אֶת תְּבוּאָתֵנוּ. וְצִוִּיתִי אֶת בִּרְכָתִי לָכֶם בַּשָּׁנָה הַשִּׁשִּׁית וְעָשָׂת אֶת הַתְּבוּאָה לִשְׁלֹשׁ הַשָּׁנִים. וּזְרַעְתֶּם אֵת הַשָּׁנָה הַשְּׁמִינִת וַאֲכַלְתֶּם מִן הַתְּבוּאָה יָשָׁן עַד הַשָּׁנָה הַתְּשִׁיעִת עַד בּוֹא תְּבוּאָתָהּ תֹּאכְלוּ יָשָׁן. וְהָאָרֶץ לֹא תִמָּכֵר לִצְמִתֻת כִּי לִי הָאָרֶץ כִּי גֵרִים וְתוֹשָׁבִים אַתֶּם עִמָּדִי.

- **It is not clear as to why the Sabbatical year is to be observed. Is it for the sake of the land, so that it can revitalize itself by lying fallow? Or is the point to reassert God's ownership of the land by periodically withdrawing permission for human beings to use it? Perhaps it is to allow the land a periodic return to its wild, "created" state. Or is it for some other reason? The Torah says specifically that the laws of the sabbatical year would apply when the Israelites "enter the land that I give you" - that is to say, the land of Israel. What does the sabbatical year have to do with North Dakota?**

- **According to the passage, to whom does the land belong? How does the sabbatical year remind us of this? How can we reflect this belief in our daily lives?**

* * * *

The following is taken from Samson Rafael Hirsch's (1808-1888) commentary to the Torah. Rabbi Hirsch was a very prominent and influential advocate for the renewal of traditional Judaism in Europe. In this passage he comments on Leviticus 25:34, which deals with the leaving of fifteen hundred feet of uncultivated land around each of the cities inhabited by the Levites in the biblical period.

And the fields of the common land surrounding their cities shall not be sold for it is a possession for them for all time. (Lev. 25:34)

וּשְׂדֵה מִגְרַשׁ עָרֵיהֶם לֹא יִמָּכֵר כִּי אֲחֻזַּת עוֹלָם הוּא לָהֶם.

Hirsch's comment: *The cities which...were to be given to the Levites, extended...2,000 cubits in every direction, of which the inner 1,000 cubits...were called* migrash ha-ir. *This "common" area, immediately surrounding the city, was an open space reserved for the animals, moveable possessions and for the other amenities of the lives of the citizens, such as a public laundry. The outer 1,000 cubits were fields and vineyards (Sotah 27b). So that the whole domain of a city consisted of* ir (city), migrash (commons) *and* sadeh (field).

Now here it says: "And the fields of the common land surrounding their cities shall not be sold..." [N]ot only is the property not to be estranged from its original owner, but also not from its original status... the field may not be converted to a free open space; the common [free open space may] not [be converted], by being plowed and sown, into a field (Baba Batra 24b) or by being built on, into the city, and equally so, not the city into a field or open space... because it was given to them as their possession for all time; therefore at no particular contemporary time has anyone the right to make any alteration to it. No present moment has the sole disposition of it, all future times have equal claim to it, and in the same condition that it has been received from the past is it to be handed on to the future.

[A]nd, according to [Rambam], this applies not only to walled cities but to every city in Israel.

[C]learly these laws establish the greatest possible upkeep of an "urban population occupied with agriculture"

as the predominant fundamental characteristic type of the Nation. It places an obstacle to the growth of large cities at the expense of the surrounding country which otherwise is so very prevalent. Not even the open spaces of the city, or any part of it, may be used as building sites. **If the population of a city grows too dense, new cities must be founded on sites which have not been used for agricultural purposes....**

- **According to the passage, why must open space be preserved in a city? Does your town have open spaces? What are they used for?**

* * * *

From **Kohelet Rabbah**, **Chapter 7**, a collection of *midrashim* from the period of the Talmud:

When God created the first human beings, God took them around the Garden, pointing out the trees. God said to the humans, "Look how beautiful and delightful are all these things I've made, and I've made them all for you. **Be careful that you do not ruin my world, because if you ruin it, no one will come along to set it right again.**

בְּשָׁעָה שֶׁבָּרָא הַקָּדוֹשׁ בָּרוּךְ הוּא אֶת אָדָם הָרִאשׁוֹן נְטָלוֹ וְהֶחֱזִירוֹ עַל כָּל אִילָנֵי גַּן עֵדֶן וְאָמַר לוֹ רְאֵה מַעֲשַׂי כַּמָּה נָאִים וּמְשֻׁבָּחִין הֵן וְכָל מַה שֶׁבָּרָאתִי בִּשְׁבִילְךָ בָּרָאתִי. תֵּן דַּעְתְּךָ שֶׁלֹא תְקַלְקֵל וְתַחֲרִיב אֶת עוֹלָמִי, שֶׁאִם קִלְקַלְתָּ אֵין מִי שֶׁיְּתַקֵּן אַחֲרֶיךָ.

- **Was the world really made for us, or were we made for it? Or were we, perhaps, made for each other?**

- **What does "no one will come along to set it right again" mean?**

- **Do human beings bear sole responsibility for the quality of life on Earth?**

- **Are we capable of bearing that responsibility?**

- **The critical question is: Does "Do not ruin my world" mean leave it as it is? Is land untouched by human activity always better than "human territory" in some way, or can we actually improve on the world we've been given by making intelligent use of its potential?**

21

- *What was Rabbi Schein's response to the question: Does the Torah place any value on leaving land untouched by human activity?*

GROUP ACTIVITY

- Draw a quick sketch of an "ideal" planned town. Where will people live, work, and spend leisure time? What services do they require (fire departments, schools, hospitals, etc.)? How will these be located?

  What percentage of "undeveloped land" did you leave? Do you know of similar debates in your own hometown? How would you have resolved such a debate?

- List below elements of the natural world (animals, plants, natural materials) that seem to have no purpose. What purpose can you suggest for them?

  ITEM   SUGGESTED PURPOSE

  _____

  _____

  _____

  _____

  _____

  _____

May we permit gentiles to hunt on our land?
What are our obligations to the animals we are raising for slaughter?

3 Nisan, 5664

Honored Rabbi, Our Teacher, Rabbi Schein,

Peace and blessings to you and your family. Thank
you for your most recent letter. We have planted
our crops in accordance with your directions, and
the fields all around us are now thick carpets of
green. As the fields come to life with new growth,
we feel as if we are witnessing a miracle. With
God's help, we will have a harvest sufficient to our
needs for the coming year.

However, we remain beset by many practical
problems that frustrate and divide us. We hold a
wide variety of opinions concerning these problems.
Though we are all committed to living Jewishly and
creating an exemplary community, we are far from
being of one mind concerning how this is to be
done. And so we turn to you for help.

The following are two questions that are currently
troubling us. As you will see, these questions are
related but not identical. Our **first question** is:

Recently, we were asked by a group of gentile   **Sefer Hasidim 666-667**
neighbors if they could hunt on our property this
coming fall. None of the members of our own
community are interested in hunting. We
understand that animals killed with guns are
t'reifah [not kosher]. We all remain committed to
kashrut and would not eat such meat, nor would
any of us take pleasure in killing an animal for
sport. But we are not in agreement concerning
whether the foregoing is all the *halachah* has to say
about the matter, or whether we are in fact not

23

only forbidden to eat such meat, but are also obligated not to assist others in killing animals in this way. The matter is further complicated by our neighbors' willingness to pay us for the use of our land for this purpose. We are in desperate need of this additional income, and are thus at a loss concerning how to proceed.

Nodah B'Yihudah, Yoreh Deah, #10

As for our **second question**, we can state is this way:

Several members of our community have suggested that we attempt to raise cattle in addition to planting crops. However, some of our members have contended that if we do so, it should only be for the purpose of kosher slaughter. One particularly tender-hearted fellow has gone so far as to maintain that the *sh'hitah* [slaughtering process] presently being done at the large stock yards in Omaha and Chicago, where our cattle would be sent, is not *kasher*, since it is done on such a large scale and with so little regard given to the condition of the animals before, during and after the *sh'hitah*. Once again, we are unsure about what to do. What does the *halachah* indicate concerning our responsibilities toward the animals we would be raising? May you be blessed for whatever counsel you can afford us. Your words are our light and support. *Hag Kasher v'sameah* [a kosher and happy holiday] to you and your family.

Baba Metsia 85a

Moreh N'vuchim 2:48

Tomer D'vorah chapter III

A. and H. Tevelmann

* * * *

<h2 align="center">TEXTS CITED</h2>

Text cited by Rabbi Schein in response to question #1: "Are we obligated not to assist others in killing animals in this way?"

From *Sefer Hasidim* (paragraphs 666 and 667), by Rabbis Meir and Y'hudah of Rothenberg, Germany (13th-14th centuries):

24

Any act that causes another pain is punished, even if it is pain needlessly caused to an animal, as, for instance, if one were to load it with more that it could bear, and then beat it when it couldn't walk. Ultimately, one will be called to account for such behavior, for the mitzvah not to cause pain to animals comes directly from the Torah.... The descendants of Noah were not given dominion over animals, whereas the first human beings, who were not allowed to eat meat to satisfy their hunger, were given dominion [over the world; Genesis 1:28-29]. But the descendants of Noah, who are allowed to eat meat to satisfy their hunger, have not been given dominion....

- **Is having "dominion" and having animals "fear and dread" human beings the same thing? If not, how do they differ?**

- **In place of the "dominion" with which the first human beings were blessed, Noah is told that humans may now eat meat, but that animals, in turn, will "fear and dread" his descendants (Genesis 9:2). Why the changes?**

- **Which is the better blessing -- "dominion" over the other creatures, or their "fear and dread" of us? Do human beings *need* dominion over the world? What about dominion over the bacteria and viruses of the microscopic world?**

  A person who doesn't need to eat meat and who knows that the meat would be left to rot because it is not needed, must not slaughter the animal. To do so would be a transgression of bal tash'hit. However, if the hide is needed, it is permitted (to slaughter the animal).

- **When the slaughtering is done on a mass scale, how can one ever be sure of what will become of the meat and hides. What does "need" mean? Do all people have the same needs? Who decides?**

* * * *

From *Noda B'Y'hudah* (*Yoreh Deah*, #10); collected responsa of Rabbi Yehezkiel Landau, Poland, 18th Century:

Question: A question has been asked of me concerning a certain individual upon whom God has bestowed

מכתבו קבלתי ואם אינני הכירו ולא ידענא
ליה אך אשר בא לשאול שאילתא ומשתעי

generous holdings. He now owns villages and forests in which all sorts of forest creatures roam. Is it permissible for him to go hunting for game with a gun, or is it forbidden for a Jew to do this, either because we are forbidden to cause needless pain to animals, or because we are forbidden to wantonly destroy any useful thing?

Answer: [W]hen a human being needs to use a living thing, the category of "not causing pain to an animal" does not apply. Furthermore, this category only applies to the pain or comfort of a **living** animal. It does not apply to the **killing** of domestic or wild animals, or any other creature. [On the other hand,] if we approach the matter in terms of the prohibition against wanton destruction rather than the prohibition against causing pain to animals, one must assume that this person would make use of the hide and is, therefore, not doing this in a wantonly destructive manner....Up until this point we have been speaking in terms of the law.

בלישנא דחכמתא הנני משיב לכל שואל. ושורש שאלתו איש אחד אשר זכהו משם בנחלה רחבה ויש לו כפרים ויערות אשר ביערות תרמוש כל אותו יער אם מותר לו לילך בעצמו לירות בקנה שריפה לצוד ציד או אם אסור לישראל לעשות דבר זו אי משום צער בעלי חיים אי משום בל תשחית...

...שכל דבר שיש בו צורך להאדם לית ביה משום לצעב"ח וגם לא שייך צעב"ח (צער בעלי חיים) אלא לצערו ולהניחו בחיים אבל להמית בהמות וחיות וכל מיני בעלי חיים לית ביה משום צעב"ח וכן מוכח בחולין דף ז' ע"ב עקרנא להו איכא צעב"ח קטלנא להו איכא משום בל תשחית הרי אף שהשיב לו על עקרנא דאיכא צעב"ח אעפ"כ אמר קטלנא להו. וא"כ אין בנדון שאלתו משום צעב"ח, ומשום בל תשחית ודאי ליכא דהרי נהנה בעור וגם אינו עושה דרך השחתה...והנה עד כה דברנו מצד הדין.

- **Hasn't the question been answered at this point? Why does Rabbi Landau continue? He seems to be going "beyond the line of the law."**

However, I am taken aback by the main point of the question. The only hunters we find [mentioned in the Torah] are Nimrod and Esau. This is not the way of Abraham, Isaac and Jacob. How can a Jew kill an animal with his own hand for no other reason than to pass the time hunting?....[It is true that] non-domesticated wild animals tend to be dangerous and so even on Shabbat it is permitted to

ואמנם מאד אני תמה על גוף הדבר ולא מצינו איש ציד רק ליד בנמרוד ובעשו ואיך זה דרכי בני אברהם יצחק ויעקב...ואין ימית איש ישראלי בידים בעלי חיים בלי שום צורך רק לגמור חמדת זמנו להתעסק בצידה...וא"כ אותן שלא נתגדלו בבתים אינם בני תרבות ודרכן להזיק והרי אפילו בשבת עכ"פ מותר לדרסן לפי תומו...ואמנם גם זה אינו ענין לנדון דידן

trample them under foot until dead....However, this is not relevant to the issue at hand, since in this latter case we have in mind an animal that enters an area where human beings are living...but to chase after them in the forest, which is where they live, when they are not in the habit of entering areas where human beings are living - this is no mitzvah; it is simply uncontrolled appetite.

דהתם כשבאו לישוב במקום בני אדם...אבל לרדוף אחריהם ביערות מקום מעונתן כשאין רגילין לבוא לישוב אין כאן מצוה ואין כאן רק לרדוף אחר תאות לבו...

- **How is this idea related to the point made in Sefer Hasidim that when the Torah gave permission to eat meat, "dominion" over other creatures was taken away from us?**

- **Is this why Rabbi Landau says that just as animals should not trespass on the human domain, so too, we have no right to trespass on theirs?**

If a person needs to do this -- making a living by hunting -- it is not a matter of cruelty, inasmuch as we slaughter cattle and other animals as well as fowl, and kill fish, to serve the needs of human beings. It makes no difference whether one is speaking of a kosher animal whose meat may be eaten, or an unkosher animal whose hides may be sold to support oneself. All animals are available to us for the purpose of serving human needs. But one who does not need to support oneself in this way, and has no intention of making a living by doing this, is behaving cruelly.

...ומי שהוא איש הצריך לזה ופרנסתו מצידה כזו בזה לא שייך אכזריות והרי שוחטין בהמות וחיות ועופות וממיתים דגים לצורך האדם ומה לי טהורים שיאכל מבשרם ומה לי טמאים שיאכל ויפרנס עצמו מדמי עורותיהן וכל בעלי חיים ניתנו לאדם לכל צרכיו, אבל מי שאין זה לצורך פרנסתו ואין עיקר כוונתו כלל בשביל פרנסתו הוא אכזריות.

- **Did this mean that the Tevelmanns were obligated to ask their neighbors *why* they hunted, and what would become of the meat and hides?**

- **What was Rabbi Schein's response to the question: May we permit gentiles to hunt on our land?**

* * * *

Texts cited by Rabbi Schein in response to question #2: "What does the *halachah* indicate concerning our responsibilities toward the animals we would be raising?"

From *Moreh Nevuchim* [Guide of the Perplexed], a philosophical commentary on the *Tanach* by Moses Maimonides (often called the Rambam), twelfth century, Egypt.

> *It is necessary that the killing of animals be regulated by* halachah, *inasmuch as the natural food of human beings consists of plants and the flesh of animals...Since, therefore, the desire to procure good food requires the killing of animals, the* halachah *requires that the death of the animal should be the easiest. It is not permitted to torment the animal by cutting the throat in a clumsy manner, by poleaxing [stunning an animal with a butcher's ax, which is an ax with a hammer at the back], or by cutting off a limb while the animal is alive.*

> *It is also forbidden to kill an animal and its young on the same day (Lev. 22:28), in order that people should be restrained and prevented from killing the two together in such a manner that the young is slain in the sight of the mother; for the pain of the animals under such circumstances is very great. There is no difference in this case between the pain of a human being and the pain of other living beings, since the love and tenderness of the mother for her young is not produced by reasoning, but by imagination, and this faculty exists not only in human beings but in most living beings....*

- **Could one be certain, amidst the noise and confusion of a large slaughterhouse, where hundreds of animals are slaughtered each day, that suffering of this sort would not occur?**

- **What is Maimonides suggesting as to similarities between human beings and animals?**

* * * *

From the Babylonian Talmud, tractate *Baba Metsia* 85a; concerning two incidents in the life of Rabbi *Y'hudah ha-Nasi* (c. 150-225 c.e.)

[How did Rabbi Y'hudah ha-Nasi's actions result in his being subject to severe suffering?] A calf that was being led to slaughter hid under the hem of Rabbi Y'hudah's robe and cried. He said to it: "Go! This is what you were created for!"

They said [in Heaven]: "Since he had no compassion for a creature, he himself will suffer." But it was also through his actions that he was relieved of his suffering. One day Rabbi Y'hudah's servant was sweeping the house. She came upon some mice and was about to sweep them out. He said to her: "God's compassion is extended to everything that God has made." They said [in Heaven]: "Since he has had compassion, compassion will be shown to him."

דְּרַבִּי עַל יְדֵי מַעֲשֶׂה בָּאוּ וְעַל יְדֵי מַעֲשֶׂה הָלְכוּ. עַל יְדֵי מַעֲשֶׂה בָּאוּ מַאי הִיא? דְּהַהוּא עֶגְלָא דַּהֲווֹ קָא מַמְטוּ לֵיהּ לִשְׁחִיטָה, אֲזַל תַּלְיָא לְרֵישֵׁיהּ בְּכַנְפֵיהּ דְּרַבִּי וְקָא בָּכֵי; אֲמַר לֵיהּ: זֵל לְכָךְ נוֹצַרְתָּ; אֲמַרִי: הוֹאִיל וְלָא קָא מְרַחֵם לֵיתוּ עֲלֵיהּ יִסּוּרִין. וְעַל יְדֵי מַעֲשֶׂה הָלְכוּ, יוֹמָא חַד הֲוָה קָא כָּנְשָׁא אַמְתֵיהּ דְּרַבִּי בֵּיתָא, הֲוָה שַׁדְיָא בְּנֵי כַּרְכֻּשְׁתָּא וְקָא כָּנְשָׁא לְהוּ, אֲמַר לָהּ שַׁבְקִינְהוּ, כְּתִיב: וְרַחֲמָיו עַל כָּל מַעֲשָׂיו; אֲמַרִי: הוֹאִיל וּמְרַחֵם נְרַחֵם עֲלֵיהּ.

* * * *

From *Tomer D'vorah* (part III), a mystical treatise by Rabbi Mosheh Cordovero, Ts'fat, Israel, sixteenth century.

> One should show compassion to all things that have been created. One should not take them for granted or wantonly destroy them, for Divine Wisdom extends to every created thing alike, whether it is a plant, an animal or a human being, and for this reason we are warned against taking food for granted. And thus, just as Divine Wisdom does not take anything for granted, and everything is made through it (as it is written) "You made them all with wisdom" (Psalm 104), so too, human beings should be compassionate toward all of God's creation.

> This is why Rabbeinu haKodesh [Rabbi Y'hudah ha-Nasi, compiler of the Mishnah] was punished, seeing as he did not take pity on a calf that hid by him. But being merciful can protect one against a severe verdict. Thus when Rabbeinu ha-Kodesh had compassion for a mouse

(as it says, "God's compassion is extended to all that God has made" Psalm 145), he was saved from any further suffering as a result of that severe verdict.

Thus one must not take anything for granted, for all things are the product of wisdom. One should not needlessly uproot a plant, nor needlessly kill a living creature, but allow them a painless death with a knife that has been carefully examined, so as to be as compassionate as possible.

This is the rule: Mercy for all things so as not to destroy them is a matter of wisdom, except when one raises the status of a thing by eating it, i.e., from vegetable to animal and from animal to human. Then it is permissible to uproot a plant and kill a living creature, committing a negative act that nevertheless leads to a positive outcome.

- **Cordevero appears to believe that animals occupy a higher rung on the ladder of life that does plant life, and that human beings occupy a higher rung than animals. Why did he believe this?**

- **How does this "rule" compare with the rule in Noda B'Y'hudah that the test of whether taking an animal's life is justified has to do with whether or not it is needed? Which is the better standard?**

- ***What was Rabbi Schein's response to the question: What does the halachah indicate concerning our responsibilities towards the animals we would be raising?***

May we limit the number of children we bear, if we fear being able to care for them all?

10 Sivan, 5664

Honored Rabbi, Our Teacher, Rabbi Schein,

Our fields are now filled with new growth. In the evening, we sometimes sit outside our front door to better catch the cooling breezes. As we look out over the fields we shake our heads at the wonder of it all. Though we have told you of the awful desolation we feel in this place, one sometimes senses a tender beauty here as well.

But along with our crops, our community is growing as well. Since we last wrote to you we have been blessed with the birth of eight babies: Naomi, Yosi, Davi, Haggai, Yaacov, Gabriel, Miriam and Rafael! Every corner of our community has been blessed by these arrivals. Yosi is the first-born of a lovely couple married just last year, while Miriam is the "daughter of the old age" of a couple in their late forties. All the children are healthy, thank God! As you can well imagine, they are the light of our lives. Their shining faces and laughter are the sweetest sights and sounds in this lonely place.

However, this blessing, like so many others we have enjoyed, raises questions for us as well. In particular, we are now asking ourselves: Is there such a thing as too many children? As much as we love them, each new mouth we must feed places every more stress on our limited resources. If we are to show restraint in any of the areas we have already written to you about, we simply cannot afford to have more and more children.

31

But many of us feel that "afford" is a strange word to use when it comes to having children. Is there any sense in calculating the "costs" and "benefits" of a human life? And even if such a calculation could be made, the great joy each birth brings to the community would certainly have to be calculated as well. How could one calculate the value of such joy? Certainly it would outweigh almost any "cost" charged against it.

And so our question: May we set limits on the size of our our population for fear that we would be unable to feed, clothe and shelter a larger community, or would doing so constitute a rejection of God's blessing that we "be fruitful and multiply?" And how would we even begin to decide which of our families would be restricted in this regard, and by what means?

Genesis 1:28

M. Y'bamot 6:6

Sotah 12a

We wish you all good things, and await your learned reply.

A. and H. Tevelmann

TEXTS CITED

Texts cited by Rabbi Schein in response to the question: "Would controlling the birth rate in our community for economic reasons be a rejection of God's blessing that we 'be fruitful and multiply?'"

Genesis 1:28:

God blessed them and said to them, "Be fruitful and multiply. Fill the Earth and subdue it. Rule over the fish in the sea and the birds in the sky, and all the living things that creep upon the Earth."

וַיְבָרֶךְ אֹתָם אֱלֹקִים וַיֹּאמֶר לָהֶם אֱלֹקִים
פְּרוּ וּרְבוּ וּמִלְאוּ אֶת הָאָרֶץ וְכִבְשֻׁהָ וּרְדוּ
בִּדְגַת הַיָּם וּבְעוֹף הַשָּׁמַיִם וּבְכָל חַיָּה הָרֹמֶשֶׂת
עַל הָאָרֶץ.

- **Until the last century or so, it must have seemed unbelievable that human beings might actually be able to "fill the Earth and subdue it." For most of human history the world and its dangers had the upper hand, but it now appears as if human beings really are beginning to dominate much of creation. If this is the case, perhaps this blessing should be revised to reflect a new reality.**

* * * *

From the Mishnah, Tractate *Y'bamot*, chapter 6, Mishnah 6:

A person is not free from the responsibility for being fruitful and multiplying until that person has two children. The House of Shammai says, "Two males." The House of Hillel says, "A male and a female," as it says in the Torah: "They were created as a male and a female" (Genesis 5:2)...Men are commanded to be fruitful and multiply, but not women. Rabbi Yohanan ben Baroka says, "The text refers to both males and females: "God blessed them, and said to them, 'Be fruitful and multiply.'"

לֹא יִבָּטֵל אָדָם מִפְּרִיָּה וּרְבִיָּה אֶלָּא אִם כֵּן יֵשׁ לוֹ בָנִים. בֵּית שַׁמַּאי אוֹמְרִים, שְׁנֵי זְכָרִים; וּבֵית הִלֵּל אוֹמְרִים, זָכָר וּנְקֵבָה, שֶׁנֶּאֱמַר, זָכָר וּנְקֵבָה בְּרָאָם (בראשית ה:ב)...הָאִישׁ מְצֻוֶּה עַל פְּרִיָּה וּרְבִיָּה אֲבָל לֹא הָאִשָּׁה. רַבִּי יוֹחָנָן בֶּן בְּרוֹקָא אוֹמֵר עַל שְׁנֵיהֶם הוּא אוֹמֵר וַיְבָרֶךְ אוֹתָם אֱלֹקִים. וַיֹּאמֶר לָהֶם, פְּרוּ וּרְבוּ.

• **Does this mean that the ideal situation would be for everyone to be a parent of at least two children, rather than a situation where some families choose to have many children while others have none? Why this preference for spreading the responsibility for child-bearing throughout the community?**

• **What if a person has four daughters and no sons? Should that person continue to bear children until a son is born?**

* * * *

From the Babylonian Talmud, Tractate *Sotah*, page 12a; a *midrash* on the circumstances of Moses' birth:

Amram [Moses' father] was the most prominent man of his generation. When he heard of Pharaoh's order that "Every male born to the Israelites is to be thrown into the Nile," he said, "Our struggle is in vain," and he divorced his wife. Then all the other men divorced their wives.

עַמְרָם גְּדוֹל הַדּוֹר הָיָה, כֵּיוָן (שֶׁרָאָה שֶׁאָמַר) פַּרְעֹה הָרָשָׁע "כָּל הַבֵּן הַיִּלוֹד הַיְאֹרָה תַּשְׁלִיכֻהוּ" אָמַר: לַשָּׁוְא אָנוּ עֲמֵלִין, עָמַד וְגֵירֵשׁ אֶת אִשְׁתּוֹ. עָמְדוּ כּוּלָּן וְגֵירְשׁוּ אֶת

33

His daughter said to him, "Father, your decree is harsher than Pharaoh's. Pharaoh's decree only concerns the males, but your decree concerns males and females. Pharaoh's decree only concerns this world, but your decree concerns this world and the world to come. And that wicked Pharaoh! -- It is not at all certain that his decree will stand. But you are a righteous person. Your decree will surely stand. [Amram] then took back his wife, and all the other men took back their wives.

נְשׁוֹתֵיהֶן. אָמְרָה לוֹ בִּתּוֹ: אַבָּא, קָשָׁה גְּזֵירָתְךָ יוֹתֵר מִשֶּׁל פַּרְעֹה. שֶׁפַּרְעֹה לֹא גָזַר אֶלָּא עַל הַזְּכָרִים, וְאַתָּה גָּזַרְתָּ עַל הַזְּכָרִים וְעַל הַנְּקֵיבוֹת, פַּרְעֹה לֹא גָזַר אֶלָּא בָּעוֹלָם הַזֶּה וְאַתָּה בָּעוֹלָם הַזֶּה וְלָעוֹלָם הַבָּא, פַּרְעֹה הָרָשָׁע סָפֵק מִתְקַיֶּימֶת גְּזֵירָתוֹ סָפֵק אֵינָהּ מִתְקַיֶּימֶת, אַתָּה צַדִּיק בְּוַדַּאי שֶׁגְּזֵירָתְךָ מִתְקַיֶּימֶת, שֶׁנֶּאֱמַר "וְתִגְזַר אֹמֶר וְיָקָם לָךְ". עָמַד וְהֶחֱזִיר אֶת אִשְׁתּוֹ, עָמְדוּ כֻּלָּן וְהֶחֱזִירוּ אֶת נְשׁוֹתֵיהֶן.

- **Amram seems to mean that Pharaoh's policies made it futile, perhaps even cruel, to continue building families and raising children. This midrash argues against such an attitude. But what right do we have to bring innocent children into terrible circumstances -- be they political, economic, or environmental?**

- **What was Rabbi Schien's response to the question: May we limit the number of children we bear, if we fear we will be unable to care for them all?**

GROUP ACTIVITY

- Re-enact the discussion between Amram and his daughter, filling out details of the story. If you were in that situation, how would you have decided to behave? To have children, even though they might be killed? To not have children? Can our world afford children today?

- As an individual or a class, list the advantages and disadvantages for the situations listed, for the groups of people listed in the following chart:

HAVING MORE THAN TWO CHILDREN

	ADVANTAGES	DISADVANTAGES
Family		
Community		
The Jewish People		
The Entire World		

* * * *

HAVING NO CHILDREN

	ADVANTAGES	DISADVANTAGES
Family		
Community		
The Jewish People		
The Entire World		

**What if we must work on the *Shabbat* to harvest the crops?
Is there a connection between the *Shabbat* we try
to observe, and the land we must till?**

13 Elul, 5664

Honored Rabbi, Our Teacher, Rabbi Schein,

Peace and blessings to you and your family.

When we first wrote to you, some seven months
ago, our fields were covered by an endless sea of
snow. Today, as we write, we are surrounded by
swaying waves of ripe grain. We have witnessed
with our own eyes God's drawing of bread from the
earth, and for this miracle we give thanks with our
whole hearts and souls.

Two weeks ago, a traveling photographer passed
through these parts and prevailed upon us to
purchase several photos. We are sending you two
of them. In one you see us standing in the midst of
the tall stalks of grain we will, God willing, soon
harvest. In the other, we are standing in front of
the community's barn. It isn't much to look at, but
it has served us well, providing protection for the
animals, a dry place for their feed, and space for a
workshop and communal office. And now we are
about to bring in a bountiful harvest. But recently
a question has arisen that gives us great concern:

Our gentile neighbors tell us that when the time
comes to harvest the crop, we must not delay, lest
foul weather damage or destroy it. You may have
guessed by now what our concern is: What if the
optimum time for harvesting our fields falls on one
of the upcoming *yamim tovim* [holidays] or
*Shabbat*ot? May we proceed with the harvest, or
must we leave our crops in the fields, even though

**Hirsch's *Judaism
Eternal*, pp. 26-31**

**Shulchan Aruch,
Orach Hayyim 245**

37

they might be damaged or deteriorate before we could get to them? What good would the observance of a *yom tov* or *Shabbat* be under such circumstances?

We await, as always, your guidance. May the coming year be a sweet one for you and your family, a year in which you reap a hundred-fold for all the kindness you have shown us.

A. and H. Tevelmann

TEXTS CITED

Texts cited by Rabbi Schein in response to the question: "What if the optimum time for harvesting our fields falls on one of the upcoming *Yamim Tovim* or on *Shabbat*?"

The following is taken from the book *Judaism Eternal* by Samson Rafael Hirsch (1808-1888). Rabbi Hirsch was a very active and influential spokesperson for the renewal of traditional Judaism in nineteenth century Europe.

> *...take heed that your political and economic life does not banish God from your heart, that you do not come to imagine that God sends manna for every soul, whether young or old, only in the wilderness, but in your organized social life, you alone, with your intellect, your strength, your mastery of life, are the provider of manna...For six days cultivate the earth and rule it!....*

> *But the seventh day is the Sabbath of the Lord thy God. On the seventh day let the husbandman forsake his plow, the reaper his scythe, the miller his mill, the baker his oven, to the spinner his spindle, the weaver his spool, the hunter his net, the tanner his pit, the furnaceman his fire, the sculptor his chisel, the trader his business, and let everyone remember Him from Whom he derives the intellect and strength, the insight and skill, to master it; Who has formed the materials, created the forces, laid down the laws which human intellect turns to account for its own use....And let him lay his productions and materials, his world and himself as holy sacrifices on the altar of Him who created heaven and earth, and who rested on the seventh day and blessed and sanctified it.*

And finally let him therefore realize that the Creator of old is the living God of today, who watches every man and every human effort, to see how man uses or abuses the world loaned to him and the forces bestowed upon him....

In what way does man rule and control the earth? Primarily in his ability to fashion all things in the environment to his own purposes. We use the earth for building materials and to grow food. We use plants and animals for food and clothing....

When the seventh day comes, by Divine command man ceases this creative control. In this way we acknowledge that we have no rights of ownership or authority over the world, other than those granted by God to Whom everything belongs.

- **Rabbi Schein would say that *Shabbat* returns "nature" to "creation." Why is that important?**

* * * *

From Rabbi Yosef Karo's *Shulḥan Aruch*, written in the latter half of the sixteenth century in Ts'fat, a small town in northern Israel. The *Shulḥan Aruch* was intended to serve as a concise halachic guide for daily Jewish living.

ישראל ועכו״ם שיש להם שדה או תנור או מרחץ או רחיים של מים בשותפו׳ או שהם שותפין בחנות בסחורה אם התנו מתחלה בשעה שבאו להשתתף שיהיה שכר השבת לעכו״ם לבדו. אם מעט ואם הרבה ושכר יום אחד כנגד יום השבת לישראל לבדו מותי׳. ואם לא התנו בתחל׳ כשיבואו לחלוק נוטל עכו״ם שכר השבתו׳ כולם והשאר חולקים אותו. ואם לא היה שכר השבת ידוע יטול העכו״ם לבדו שביעית השכר וחולקים השאר.

If a Jew and a non-Jew are partners in the ownership of a field, or oven, or bathhouse... it is permitted for them to agree from the outset that whatever profit is made on Shabbat will belong to the non-Jew alone, whether it is great or small, and the profits from another day of the week in place of Shabbat, will belong to the Jew alone. If they don't have such an agreement from the outset, when it comes time to split the profits, the non-Jew receives all profits made on Shabbat and they split the rest. (Orach Hayyim 245)

- **It seems that Rabbi Schein intended to suggest that if the farmers entered into a partnership with their non-Jewish neighbors, they could be assured of not winding up without an income for the year as a result** of not harvesting their crops on Yom Tov or *Shabbat*. But if every Jew did this, what would happen to *Shabbat*?

- What would become of S. R. Hirsch's idea that on *Shabbat* we must "restore the world to God" by ceasing our "creative control?" With whose position do you agree?

* * * *

The following is taken from Rabbi Mosheh Isserles' comments on the preceding passage from the *Shulḥan Aruch*. Isserles' commentary, written just a few years after the *Shulḥan Aruch* itself was completed, adapted Rabbi Karo's work, which reflected s'fardic practice, to the practices then current in central Europe, where Rabbi Isserles lived.

Some authorities allow [a Jewish and non-Jewish partner] to simply split the profits if they had no agreement at the outset. This rule applies if a great loss would otherwise be incurred. There are those who say that these rules only apply when the partners have specific days on which each of them work. However, when the two of them work together on weekdays, and only the non-Jew works on Shabbat, it is permissible to simply split all the profits, because the non-Jew is exercising his own prerogative by working on Shabbat. Therefore, the Jew is not deriving benefit through the labor of the non-Jew on Shabbat, since the responsibility for that work is not being delegated to the non-Jew.

הנה ויש מתירין השכר בדעבד אפילו לא
התנו וחלקו סתם ונ״ל דבהפסד גדול יש
לסמוך עלייהו וי״א שכל זה לא מיירי אלא
בשותפות שכל א׳. עוסק ביומו אבל
כששניהם עוסקי׳ ביחד כל ימי החול
ובשבת עוסק העכו״ם לבדו מותי לחלוק
עמו כל השכר דעכו״ם. אדעתיה דנפשיה
קא עביד ואין הישראל נהנה במלאכתו
בשבת כיון שאין המלאכה מוטלת עליו
לעשות.

- The point about "great loss" is critical. Most people would probably agree that letting go of "creative control" of the world, at "certain times" is probably a good idea. The question is: What if by doing so, it becomes impossible for someone to make a decent living, or seriously lowers the quality of a person's life in some other way?

- Also: does "great loss" mean the same thing for the rich and the poor?

- *What was Rabbi Schein's response to the question: What if the optimum time for harvesting our fields falls on one of the upcoming yamim tovim or Shabbatot?*

GROUP ACTIVITY

- Role-play the town meeting at which a decision needs to be made about whether to harvest crops on *Shabbat*. Choose someone to play the role of Avraham Tevelmann, who will serve as chairperson for the meeting. Select 2 or 3 others to represent each side of the argument (go ahead and harvest on *Shabbat*, don't harvest at all, or hire non-Jews).

  Be sure to bring the citations Rabbi Schein has provided above into the discussion.

- In the end, what was the decision?

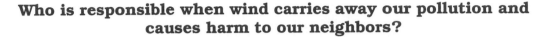
Who is responsible when wind carries away our pollution and causes harm to our neighbors?

7 Tishrei, 5665

Honored Rabbi, Our Teacher, Rabbi Schein,

Imagine our surprise when Sh'muel returned this morning from his weekly trip to Bismarck with the packages you sent. Each of the babies are now happily resting on their new blankets. The children's parents have asked us to relay their deepest appreciation to you for the gifts. One does not often come across such beautiful blankets in these parts.

But, in addition to expressing our appreciation for your generous gifts, we would also like to tell you about an issue having to do with harvesting our crops that we were compelled to resolve on our own, as there was no time to consult you. As you will recall, we were warned by our neighbors that when harvest time came, we could not afford to delay.

We believe that our resolution of the problem was in keeping with the spirit of the *halachah*, if not its particulars. Nevertheless, though the issue has been resolved, at least for the time being, we would like to know how you would have approached the problem.

Along with many of our neighbors, our community made arrangements to rent a steam-powered threshing machine to harvest our wheat. And what a machine it was! Heaps of wheat were swallowed up by the front of it, while bag after bag of grain poured out at the back. Great clouds of smoke billowed up from the steam tractor that supplied the power for the thresher, as a steady stream of chaff spewed out to the side. It rumbled and banged as it devoured the wheat, while a team of workers stood by with big sacks to catch the grain as it emerged from the machine.

It was only after two or three heaps of cut stalks had been threshed that David and Riva Freidman, whose house was located very near where the machine had been set up, came running out to the field, waving their hands and shouting furiously. The Freidmans had to fight their way through the noise and smoke and chaff, along with the excitement of the moment, to make themselves understood. They finally convinced the workers to turn off the machine. They then explained that the noise it was making was terrifying, and that their house and yard, along with the clean laundry they had just hung out to dry, were now covered with chaff and stank of smoke.

The Freidmans insisted that no more of that field, nor any of the other fields nearby, be threshed by machine. Several of the community's members began to argue with the Friedmans about the cost and inconvenience of not using the thresher, while others went over to the Freidmans' house to have a closer look at the alleged damage. The general impression of these inspectors was that the Freidmans' unhappiness was not altogether unwarranted.

The Freidmans claimed that the community was responsible for the losses they had suffered and asked that they be reimbursed. However, at the special community meeting called to consider the case, more than one person suggested that the community should not be held responsible. Several reasons for taking this position were put forward, including:

- The community cannot be held responsible for the consequences of a shifting wind that happened to carry the smoke and chaff over to the Freidmans' house.

- The Freidmans must have realized that choosing the convenience of putting their home near the fields meant that they were increasing the risk that something like this might happen.

Old Boroch (the man who was against raising cattle for slaughter and cultivating as much land as possible) laid the blame for the whole affair at the feet of the threshing machine itself. He claimed that nothing good ever came of big machines, and that any fool knows they make an awful racket, and fill the air with flying debris and terrible smells. He wound up this "d'rash" with the ringing declaration that, "The only thing more mindless than a machine is a person who's become dependent upon one!"

Following this airing of views, we got down to the business of hammering out a solution. Ultimately, it was decided that the community would offer to pay for half of the actual damage done by the chaff and smoke, plus a small reimbursement for "discomfort and inconvenience." The Freidmans accepted this offer and, we are happy to say, the harvest was completed without further mishaps.

However, having resolved the issue in this way, we are nevertheless interested in knowing if we reached a conclusion which is, in your eyes, k'halachah. Specifically:

Is a person responsible for what the wind carries from his or her property to the property of a neighbor? Can a whole community be held responsible?

M. Baba Batra 2:8

Shulhan Aruch, Hoshen Mishpat 155

Did the Freidmans have the right to demand that the harvest be continued by hand, even though the community had already paid a great deal to rent

Teshuvot Maharshach, part 2, subsection 98

45

the threshing machine? Also, can noise cause "damage?"

Please forgive us, Rabbi, for taking up so much of your time with our unending questions and concerns. The approach of *Yom Kippur* reminds each of us of our many sins, including the sin of imposing one's troubles on good-hearted friends, but we are eager to know what the Torah teaches us about these things.

This year *Yom Kippur* means something new to us as well. This year, as we begin our fast, each of our families will be more acutely aware than ever before of the mixture of miracle and hard work required to put bread on our tables. And when we celebrate *Sukkot*, we will have the great satisfaction of thanking God for a harvest which was the work of our own hands.

May this season of joy be filled with joy for you and your family.

Avraham and Hannah Tevelmann

* * * *

TEXTS CITED

Texts cited by Rabbi Schein in response to the question: "Is a person responsible for what the wind carries from his or her property to the property of a neighbor?"

This passage is taken from *Mishnah Baba Batra*, Mishnah 2:8. The *halachot* quoted here date back approximately two thousand years, if not more.

A permanent threshing floor must be no closer to a town than seventy-five feet. Nor may one make a threshing floor on one's own property unless there is a margin of seventy-five feet on every side.	מַרְחִיקִין גֹּרֶן קָבוּעַ מִן הָעִיר חֲמִשִּׁים אַמָּה. לֹא יַעֲשֶׂה אָדָם גֹּרֶן קָבוּעַ בְּתוֹךְ שֶׁלּוֹ, אֶלָּא אִם כֵּן יֶשׁ לוֹ חֲמִשִּׁים אַמָּה לְכָל רוּחַ...

- **This rule must be intended to minimize the possibility of chaff from threshed grain being carried by the wind to neighboring property --**

46

exactly the problem the Tevelmanns faced. It's interesting that the *halachah* does not distinguish between requirements for the construction of public and private threshing floors. Communities are to be held to the same standards as individuals in regard to air-born pollution.

* * * *

From Rabbi Yosef Karo's *Shulḥan Aruch*, written in the latter half of the sixteenth century in S'fat, a small town in northern Israel. The *Shulḥan Aruch* was intended to serve as a concise *halachic* guide for daily Jewish living:

If one builds a threshing floor on one's own property or digs a latrine, or does work that makes for dust, dirt, etc., it must be situated so that the dirt or smell of the latrine or the dust doesn't reach a neighbor and cause damage. Even if in the course of one's work the wind carries the dirt or shreds of flax or chaff, etc., and it reaches a neighbor, one is obligated to keep it at a distance so that it doesn't reach the neighbor and cause damage. Even if it is carried by the wind, such cases are analogous to causing damage with an arrow.

However, though one is obligated to place them at a distance, if chaff or dirt is carried by the wind and as a result damage is caused, one is not required to pay for the damage because it was the wind that enabled it to occur. [The general rule] concerning the placement of something at a distance is that if it is not placed at a distance and a neighbor is aware of this but says nothing, it is as if the neighbor has given permission [for it not being moved further away.] The neighbor cannot, at a later date, require that it be moved.

מי שעשה גורן בתוך שלו או קבע בית הכסא או מלאכה שיש בה אבק ועפר וכיוצא בהם צריך להרחיק כדי שלא יגיע העפר או ריח בית הכסא או האבק לחבירו כדי שלא יזיקו אפילו היתה הרוח הוא שמסייע אותו בעת שעושה מלאכתו ומוליכה את העפר או נעורת הפשתן והמוץ וכיוצא בהן ומגיעתן לחבירו ה"ז חייב להרחיק כדי שלא יגיעו ולא יזיקו ואפי' ע"יי רוח מצויה שכל אלו כמו שהזיקו בחיציו הן ואע"פ שהוא חייב להרחיק כל כך אם הוליכה הרוח המצויה המוץ והעפר והזיקה בהן פטור מלשלם שהרוח הוא שסייע אותו.

כל הרחקות שאמרנו אם לא הרחיק וראה חבירו ושתק ה"ז מחל ואינו יכול לחזור ולהצריכו להרחיק והוא שראה ממנו שמחל עז כגון שסייע עמו מיד או שאמר לו לעשות או שראהו שעשה בצדו בלא הרחקה ושתק ולא הקפיד על זה זכה.

47

- **One is obligated to prevent the damage from occurring, but not obligated to pay for it if it does occur. How come?**

However, in the case of damage caused by smoke, the odor of a latrine, dust, or causing the ground to vibrate, this rule does not apply. Even if a person says nothing about these activities for several years, one can, at a later date, force the owner to move it further away...Why are these particular types of damage distinguished from the others? The difference is that people cannot tolerate these kinds of damage, and one cannot forfeit one's right to be free of a chronic source of damage. However, if one sells one's right to protest one of these sources of damage, it cannot be taken back at a later date.

במה דברים אמורים בשאר נזקים חוץ הארבע שהם העשן וריח בית הכסא ואבק וכיוצא בו ונדנוד הקרקע שכל אחד מאלו אין לו חזקה ואפילו שתק כמה שנים הרי זה חוזר וכופהו להרחיק.

ולמה שינו נזקין אלו משאר נזקין לפי שאין דעתו של אדם סובלת נזקין אלו וחזקתו שאינו מוחל שהזיקו היזק קבוע ואם קנו מידו שמחל בניזקין אלו בא אינו יכול לחזור בו.

- **What does "people cannot tolerate these kinds of damages" mean?**

- **Does the last sentence mean that people may sell their right to protection from pollutants?**

- **If one cannot forfeit one's right to be free of a source of chronic damage, why does the *halachah* appear to tolerate the selling of that right?**

* * * *

Rabbi Shlomo Cohen, writing in sixteenth century Turkey, issued the following response to a question concerning industries that produce air-born pollutants. This responsum is included in a collection of Rabbi Cohen's responsa entitled *T'shuvot Maharshach (part II, subsection 98)*:

> *The damage caused to the townspeople by the vats used by the dyeing industry is extremely great and has to be considered as similar to that of smoke and bad odors. However, since the textile industry is the main basis for the livelihood of the people of this town, it is incumbent on the neighbors to suffer the damage. This is an*

on the neighbors to suffer the damage. This is an enlargement of the principle that where a person is doing work that is essential to his livelihood and that it is not possible to do elsewhere, the neighbors do not have the right to prevent it.

- **What was Rabbi Schein's response to the question: Who is responsible when wind carries away our pollution and causes harm to our neighbors? Did he agree with the decision made by the town?**

GROUP ACTIVITY

- Form a "**H**evruta:" A **H**evruta is a small group of people (usually two or three) who study texts together. Find one or two friends, and study one or all of the three texts cited by Rabbi Schein, using the Hebrew or English text provided. For each text, answer the following questions:

  - What is the legal principle explained by the passage?

  - Does this principle apply to the case of the North Dakota settlement, as explained in their letter?

  - Based on the three texts, did Rabbi Schein approve of the community's decision?

- Make a list of things your neighbors do that you find hard to tolerate. Do you have a right to ask them to stop?

Chapter VII

Yoni ponders the *Sukkah*

I lay on my back, watching patches of sky float overhead, and I think back to a bright starry evening from last *Sukkot*.

Last year I spent a whole night in our *sukkah*. It had been so cold that night that when we awoke in the morning we could see our breath in the air. Now, as I lay alone on the grass, I thought back to that morning, how we had all scrambled into the house, yelling and pushing to be first to stand over a heat vent, wrapped from head to toe in blankets and sleeping bags.

I began to think about how dependent we are on the wires and tubes that bring water and gas and electricity into our homes and carry the sewage out. And I thought about all the trucks and workers that stock the grocery shelves, where I can select to my heart's content, and eat to fullest satisfaction, without ever having to break a sweat or lift a hoe. For a moment I imagined all this apparatus, especially as represented by the electric lines and the sewage pipes, as intravenous tubes and catheters -- unsightly but essential lifelines for a body that could not function on its own.

No such lifelines sustained the *sukkah*, I thought. It stands on its own.

During the next day, when I was back in school, I made a point of telling my friends about my image of the modern home, hooked up to intravenous tubes and the like. Then I asked them:

- **"Have you ever worn something made of materials that you, or someone you knew had raised?"**

- **"Have you ever eaten food that you yourself had grown?"**

- **"Have you ever eaten food that you yourself had raised, or slaughtered?"**

- **"Or eaten fish that you caught?"**

- **"Have you ever lived in a home that you and your family actually built with your own hands?"**

Some of my friends had eaten food from their own gardens and one of them had eaten a fish she had caught, but none of them had ever done any of the other things I asked about. For that matter, neither had I.

I thought about how distant my friends and I were from the sources of our food, clothing and shelter. It seemed to me as if we were living in an "environmental intensive care unit," sustained by all sorts of machinery, high tech and otherwise. Without it all, I doubt if we could survive, so dependent are we.

How different it had been for the Tevelmanns and their friends. They had grown most of their own food, raised and slaughtered their own animals, built their own homes, sown their own clothes. Maybe their closeness to the land, to the elements, was what prompted them to display their obvious concern and care for all life.

As *Sukkot* came to an end last year, I took out my diary and spent another hour or two watching the clouds inch by. Then I wrote:

What have I learned from building a *sukkah*? I've learned that we must not only bring a bit of our homes into our *sukkot*, but we must also take something of our *sukkot* back into our homes. In the coming year I will try to make our home more fully **a piece of, and at peace with**, the environment that surrounds it. For me, that means...

- First, I will plant a vegetable garden.

- Second, I will: _____

- Then, I will: _____

- _____

- _____

- _____

- _____

Chapter VIII: Sh'aylah #6

Are there any limits to what we can build? Is enough ever enough?

2 Heshvan, 5665

Honored Rabbi, Our Teacher, Rabbi Schein,

Warm greetings from our home to yours.

We want you to know that though we sowed our fields with anxious tears we have, with God's help, harvested our crops in joy. We have completed our harvest before the arrival of a killing frost and autumn storms, and now feel reasonably prepared and secure against the terrible cold which will, once again, soon engulf us. As it says in the Psalms,

Our gates are strong,
Our children are blessed,
Our borders are peaceful,
And we are satisfied with fine wheat!

Though we will, no doubt, be faced by many more questions and problems in the years ahead, we feel that in the past year we have learned much of what we will need to know to build the community to which we aspire. You have been an unwavering source of support through this period of testing and learning. We are forever grateful to you for the guidance you have given us.

For the time being, however, we are confronted with one more question that we would ask your help in resolving. No doubt you noticed in the photos we sent to you that our buildings and farm equipment are quite old and worn. All our possessions are homely but adequate to the purposes for which they are intended.

As a result of the very bountiful crop we have recently harvested, some members of our community have begun to say that we must use our profits to build our settlement into something much finer. They are pressing us to rebuild our original buildings, construct new roads, buy more "advanced" farm machinery, build new homes, etc.

Others of us say: Should we build just because we can build, or buy things just because we can buy them? Some people might say that our farms are not so beautiful, but what does "beautiful" really mean? Isn't simplicity also beautiful? A ways west of here there is a group of people called "Hutterites." They are Christian farmers who believe that one must serve God simply. The Hutterites' homes are very plain, as is their clothing. They don't rush off to buy the latest new invention or fashion. They believe that plainness is beautiful and so choose to live "plainly." Perhaps we have something to learn from them. Then again, about 35 miles north of here there is a large Dakota Indian reservation. The people on the reservation live very simply as well, but in this case it is because the Indians' poverty leaves them no choice but to live this way. However, some people say it is the Dakotas' way, as it is the Hutterites', to live a "plain" life, and that they too would freely choose simplicity if poverty didn't force it upon them.

What about our people, Rabbi? Should we aspire to plainness and simplicity as well, or are we foolish not to capitalize on our blessings? If we do not remodel and expand now, will we be short-changing our children and undercutting their future?

On the other hand, in almost every *t'shuvah* you have sent us, you have emphasized that the Torah requires that we decide how best to use the resources of this world on the basis of an honest calculation of our true needs, and that there is often a great deal of difference between what one really *needs* and what one sometimes *wants*.

And so we turn to you once again for assistance. With our storehouses full and our homes well-stocked for the winter, our question is, for once, not about how we might prevail in our struggle for survival, but about what we do now that we have prevailed. Are there limits to human need, Rabbi Schein? Is enough ever really enough?

Shabbat 140b

**Hovot HaLevavot,
Sha'ar Heshbon
Hanefesh 3:12**

We await your reply, dear teacher and friend.

B'vrachah,

A. and H. Tevelmann

P.S. It is now twilight -- the time "between the suns." The horizon is awash in a glowing pink, but when I refocus my eyes on the window-pane just above my right shoulder the pink recedes and dozens of sparkling snow crystals appear. They cling to the window for a moment, before yielding to the warmth on the other side of the glass. It is the first snow of the winter.

"God sends down snow like wool, scattering frost like ashes; God hurls down ice crystals like crumbs; who can withstand this cold?" We have now lived one year in this strange new land. When spring comes we will, God willing, begin again. *Baruch attah ha-shem, Elokeinu Melech ha-Olam, she-hecheyanu, v'kiy-manu v'higiyanu laz'man hazeh.* [Blessed are you, Lord our God, who causes us to live, sustains us, and allows us to reach this time].

* * * *

TEXTS CITED

A text cited by Rabbi Schein in response to the question: "Should we aspire to plainness and simplicity, or are we foolish not to capitalize on our blessings?"

From the Babylonian Talmud [*Shabbat* 140b] concerning two third-century rabbis' attitudes toward the mitzvah of "*Bal tash'hit*" ("do not waste").

Rav Hisdah said, "Someone who can eat barley bread but eats wheat bread breaks the commandment 'Do not waste.'"

Rav Pappa said, "Someone who can drink beer but drinks wine breaks the commandment 'Do not waste.'"

But this is incorrect. One must first apply "Do not waste" to one's own body!

וְאָמַר רַב חִסְדָּא הַאי מַאן דְּאֶפְשָׁר לֵיהּ לְמֵיכַל נַהֲמָא דִשְׂעָרֵי וְאָכֵל דְּחִיטֵּי קָעָבַר מִשּׁוּם בַּל תַּשְׁחִית. וְאָמַר רַב פָּפָּא הַאי מַאן דְּאֶפְשָׁר לְמִישְׁתֵּי שִׁכְרָא וְשָׁתֵי חַמְרָא עוֹבֵר מִשּׁוּם בַּל תַּשְׁחִית. וְלָאו מִלְּתָא הִיא בַּל תַּשְׁחִית דְּגוּפָא עֲדִיף.

- **What is the meaning of this passage? How does it relate to the question posed by the Tevelmanns?**

From *Hovot HaLevavot, Sha'ar Heshbon HaNefesh* 3:12, of Rabbi Bahya ibn Pekudah:

It is time to carefully search one's soul when one impetuously and whole-heartedly throws oneself into the pursuit of worldly gain, investing in it one's utmost energy and keenest calculations....Such a person is like a fire that burns ever fiercer as wood is added to it....They come to count only those who can further their worldly interests as their friends, and only those who facilitate worldly gain as trustworthy companions. They look forward to the seasons when inventories can be accumulated, and then to the seasons when it can be sold. They study market conditions, the relative cost of items, and rising and falling prices. Neither heat nor cold, nor stormy seas, nor long desert journeys deter them.

חשבון האדם עם נפשו בעת המית לבו והריצותו על העולם בכל השתדלותו ותכלית תחבולותיו וסוף יכלתו...אך הוא כאש כל אשר תוסיף עצים היא מוסיפה להבה וכל לבו וכונתו מושכים אליו יומם ולילה, איננו חושב לאוהב אלא מי שיעזרהו עליו ולא רע נאמן אלא המישרהו אליו ויצפה לעתות אצור המפהרים ועתי מכירתם וצופה עניני השער וחוקר על יוקר הסחורות וזלותם ועלותם וירידתם בכל קצוי הארץ ולא יעכבהו בדרכים הרחוקים חום ולא קור ולא סער הים ולא אורך הדרך במדברות אך כל זה לתקותו שיגיע אל תכלית ואין תכלית לו ואפשר שתהיה יניעתו לריק ולא יעלה בידו כי אם הצער הארוך והטורח והעמל.

But all of this is done in the hope of reaching the end of something for which there is no end. It is even possible that all these exertions will, in the end, come to nothing, leading only to protracted pain, trouble, and travail. Thus the pious one [Solomon] asked of God that he be given only as much sustenance as he needed, keeping him from riches, which lead to excess, and from poverty, which can undermine character and learning, as he said (Proverbs 30:7-8), "I have asked two things of You: give me neither poverty nor riches, simply feed me my allotted share..."

וכן שאל החסיד מאלהיו לתת לו מן המזון די ספוקו ולהרחיק ממנו העושר המביא אל המותרות וחריש המביא אל אבדת המוסר והתורה באמרו (משלי ל) שתים שאלתי מאתך ראש ועושר אל תתן לי הטריפני לחם חקי.

- But how do we draw the line between what we *want* and what we *need*? Can we be trusted to do it for ourselves? If Rabbi Bahya is correct about the addictive character of worldly pursuits, one could conclude that each of us might turn out to be our own worst judge of what we actually need. Just look at Solomon, that "pious" man!

- Setting honest and healthy standards of need in our lives is a need in its own right, and often a tough one to fulfill. What can we use as guidelines?

- *What was Rabbi Schein's response to the question: Is enough ever enough?*

GROUP ACTIVITY

- List below examples of items you own, were given, bought for yourself, or acquired in some other way, but don't really need. Why did you buy the item? If you kept the item, why?

_____

_____

_____

_____

Chapter IX

Yoni contemplates what to do with the letters

As Mrs. Saltz worked on the translations, I continued to see the significance of the letters in terms of what they might tell me about the life and times of my great-great Grandfather. The letters were a physical link between us. Then something strange began to happen. Every few days or so, I would read or hear about some issue or problem that reminded me of the Tevelmanns and their questions. The treatment of other living creatures, population control, air quality -- I found the questions everywhere. Again and again, school assignments, magazines, conversations with friends seemed to touch on the very same themes discussed in the letters.

It was like how, sometimes, right after learning the meaning of a new word, you start finding the word everywhere, and you wonder why you hadn't noticed it before. I began to see how the Tevelmanns' questions were being raised in my world as well. It was as if the lovely antique writing, so carefully laid down some ninety years ago, had freed itself from the old, yellowed paper and was now moving about in the present.

And then, in April, Mrs. Saltz had a stroke. I visited her once in the hospital. I knew it was going to be hard to see her in such bad shape, but I was certain she'd enjoy having some company. During that visit she was able to speak a little. Her words came out slowly, somewhere between regular speech and a whisper, but they were clear enough. "Do you still have the letters?" she asked. "Yes, I do," I said. She smiled. "Don't lose them," she said. We sat quietly together for a minute or two.

I looked out the window so as not to stare at her. Sunlight was pouring in. A rectangle of light stretched across the foot of her bed. When I glanced back at Mrs. Saltz she was asleep. It became clear to me that Mrs. Saltz's illness would probably prevent her from helping me to fully understand what these letters meant. The sources that Rabbi Schein cited were too unfamiliar for me to completely grasp on my own. Who would I turn to now?

That afternoon I re-read the Tevelmanns' first letter to Rabbi Schein once again, and then began to write one of my own.

Letter to Rabbi Gordon

I was about six years old when I first met Rabbi Aharon Gordon. I still see him now as he appeared to me then, his smile reaching from one end to the other of the thickest glasses I had ever seen. As the rabbi of our congregation, he was very much involved as our family became increasingly active in the synagogue. He studied with my siblings and me for our B'nai Mitzvah, officiated at my grandmother's funeral, and was, in so many other ways, close to our family during many major moments. I always enjoyed being invited over to his home on *Shabbat* afternoons for U.S.Y. study, and we frequently took walks together in the lazy *Shabbat* afternoons of late August and early September.

In 1989 Rabbi Gordon decided to make *aliyah* with his family and they now live in Jerusalem. Though I haven't seen him in nearly three years, we have written to each other on occasion, and for many reasons, it seemed natural to write to him after the discovery of the letters.

During the years I was Rabbi Gordon's student he taught me many things. The lesson that made the most lasting impression sounds so simple it may not even strike you as worth remembering. What he told me was to remember to "**always start from where you really are.**" I told you it sounds simple, but it's not always so easy. What I think he meant by that is that we often pretend to be done with a job we've only just begun, or at least further along than we'd like to believe we are. Even more than that, we never get where we want to go if we pretend to be where we're not. Throughout our lives we have to keep asking ourselves: where are we, and which path leads from where we really are to where we should be?

I wrote to Rabbi Gordon because I needed help understanding if Rabbi Schein's notes -- his quotations from the Torah, the Talmud and the like -- have anything to tell us about "where we really are" these days. I didn't realize how much I missed him until the first of his letters arrived.

* * * *

May 4, 1991

Dear Rabbi Gordon,

Please forgive me for not writing to you for the past year or so, and for not writing in Hebrew now. I miss you very much. I understand how important making *aliyah* has been to you, but since you left, it has been somewhat awkward for me to go to services. I am gradually getting to know your

60

successor, Rabbi Liebman, and I like him a lot.
But it is different! I especially miss our *Shabbat*
walks. Are you still solving all the world's problems
on *Shabbat* walks with your students, like we used
to do on ours?

The reason I am writing to you now is that for the
past several months I have been involved in a very
interesting project. In January, I happened to find
several letters written to my great-great
grandfather, Rabbi El<u>h</u>anan Halevi Schein, from a
group of Jews who were trying to establish a
Jewish community in North Dakota at the turn of
the century. The letters were written in Yiddish.
Each includes at least one question about how they
should live their lives "so as to find favor with God
and other human beings." Around the margins of
the letters there are notes which I am quite certain
served as the basis for my great-great grandfather's
responses. (Mrs. Saltz did the translations for me.
Have you heard that she had a stroke? I visited
her today. She's really amazing.)

What I find most interesting about the letters we
have translated so far is the extent to which the
problems these people faced resemble issues that
remain very much alive today. I am also fascinated
by my great-great grandfather's efforts to solve
these problems on the basis of traditional Jewish
sources, but I don't know what to make of his
approach. This is partly because we don't have his
actual responses, just his notes. Mrs. Saltz and I
have had to put together the sources he cites on
the basis of our own reasoning. In addition, I'm
just not sure about the whole idea of looking for
solutions to modern problems in ancient sources.
As the people from North Dakota say in one of their
letters, "There are some among us who insist that
the Torah has nothing to teach us about such
things."

Sometimes I also doubt whether the Torah has
something to teach us about such things. I've read
the sources Rabbi Schein mentions in his notes

many times and, for the most part, I've been able to put them together in ways that I'd like to believe were close to what he had in mind. But even if those ancient sources were helpful to Rabbi Schein and the farmers in North Dakota, I'm not at all sure that they can help us much anymore. When we discuss issues in school that seem related to the questions raised in the letters -- questions about the environment, population control, the treatment of animals -- I hesitate to mention the letters I found, much less Rabbi Schein's notes. I guess I'm afraid that if I try to apply them to the issues we're discussing, I'll seem hopelessly out of touch. Yet I remember that you never seemed "out of touch" when you discussed a contemporary event in light of the Torah and its teachings. Perhaps, then, you can help me to understand what relevance, if any, the letters have to the "here and now." Would you be willing to look at the letters and respond to the issues they raise? Mrs. Saltz and I jotted down notes and questions of our own as we worked our way through the letters. I would like to send you those comments, too.

By the way, speaking of "here and now," do your students in Israel ask you these sorts of questions? I've grown up imagining that the Jews of Israel have really gone a long way toward creating the kind of communities the people who wrote the letters to Rabbi Schein hoped to build. One would think that Jews, living in their own land, free to live the sort of lives the great Jewish poets and philosophers dreamed about for centuries, would at least come close to building communities that "find favor with God and other human beings." Or am I lost in utopia?

I have to close for now. I know that your time is precious, but if you have a moment to respond to my questions I would really appreciate it. It would remind me of our *Shabbat* walks. Please give my regards to your family.

Kol Tuv [all the best], Yoni

Chapter X

Rabbi Gordon's initial letter

Jerusalem, 7 Iyar, 5751

Dear Yoni,

It was wonderful to hear from you. Though I have all sorts of wonderful new students here, I also miss our *Shabbat* walks.

Your letter about Rabbi Schein was fascinating. What a wonderful story! Nor am I surprised by your comments about Mrs. Saltz. I was always impressed by her. We were, however, very distressed to hear of her illness. Please wish her a *refuah shelemah -- a speedy recovery --* from our entire family.

The letter sent by that North Dakota community sounds incredible. Even more, it seems remarkably modern. What I mean is that the questions raised by the Tevelmanns and their neighbors are not unlike the sort of questions we wrestle with here in Israel all the time. Like that Dakota community, we are also striving to create a society that will reflect Jewish sensitivities and values. As we try, we find ourselves not only looking to the traditional sources for guidance, but realizing that reconciling our Jewish teachings with modern concerns can be challenging.

For example, the question you raised in your letter -- **DOES TRADITIONAL JUDAISM HAVE MUCH TO SAY ABOUT HOW WE SHOULD TREAT THE ENVIRONMENT?** -- is not so easy to answer. What I have discovered in an environmental group which I recently joined, *Hug Haaretz,* is not only that some are skeptical about what Judaism, and other western religions, can offer to the pressing ecological questions of the day, but that some actually *blame* Judaism and Christianity for our ecological predicament.

That judgment is based on the concluding passage in the Genesis account of creation:

And God said, "I will make humans in My image, after My likeness. They shall rule the fish of the sea, the birds of the sky, the cattle, the whole earth, and all that creeps on earth." And

וַיִּבְרָא אֱלֹקִים אֶת הָאָדָם בְּצַלְמוֹ בְּצֶלֶם אֱלֹקִים בָּרָא אֹתוֹ זָכָר וּנְקֵבָה בָּרָא אֹתָם. וַיְבָרֶךְ אֹתָם אֱלֹקִים וַיֹּאמֶר לָהֶם אֱלֹקִים פְּרוּ וּרְבוּ וּמִלְאוּ אֶת הָאָרֶץ וְכִבְשֻׁהָ וּרְדוּ בִּדְגַת הַיָּם וּבְעוֹף הַשָּׁמַיִם וּבְכָל חַיָּה הָרֹמֶשֶׂת עַל הָאָרֶץ.

63

God created humans in Godly image, in that image God created; male and female God created. God blessed them and God said to them: "Be fertile and increase, fill the earth and master it; and rule the fish of the sea, the birds of the sky, and all the living things that creep on earth." [Gen. 1:27-8]

The phrase פְּרוּ וּרְבוּ וּמִלְאוּ אֶת הָאָרֶץ וְכִבְשֻׁהָ וּרְדוּ -- *"Be fertile and increase; fill the earth and master it; and rule...."* has sparked much controversy among scholars.

- **Are the two Hebrew words, כִּבְשֻׁהָ and רְדוּ, to be translated as we have above, with verbs that are neutral: "*master the earth and rule...?*" Or are those Hebrew words meant to confer on human beings something different, that is better translated this way: "*Conquer the earth and subjugate it?*"**

- **What difference do you see in these two translations? Does *"master"* imply a different relationship to the earth than *"conquer?"* Is there a difference between being told to *"rule"* rather than *"subjugate"* the creatures? From your study of Torah, which translation seems most consistent with the Torah's general view of the relationship between human beings and the rest of creation?**

While these may seem to be technical questions, Yoni, or maybe even trivial, the precise meaning of these verses, and their interpretations through the ages, have been hotly debated by modern thinkers. Basically, there are two sharply divergent views about the meaning of these verses and their relationship to our contemporary environmental condition.

One side maintains that this passage has shaped Western thinking, lulling human beings into believing that both the earth and all that live upon it are subject to human use. Lynn White, Jr., a specialist in the history of science and technology at the University of California, outlined such a position in a famous essay entitled "The Historic Roots of Our Ecologic Crisis" [*Science*, 155 (10 March 1967), 1203-1207]. In the beginning of the article, he argues that those Genesis verses convey the clear implication of humanity's right to exploit the earth. This exploitative ethic has sanctioned the way we human beings now relate to the earth, providing us with a rationale from the highest source -- the Bible -- that we may use the earth as we wish. In fact, White believes that this notion of human beings as the "masters" of creation is so prevalent in Western thinking that we are not even aware of the way it has shaped our thinking and behavior. This is how White says it:

> *The present increasing disruption of the global environment...cannot be understood historically apart from distinctive attitudes toward nature which are deeply grounded in Christian dogma. The fact that most people do not think of these attitudes as Christian is irrelevant. No new set of basic values has been accepted in our society to displace those of Christianity. Hence we shall continue to have a worsening ecologic crisis until we reject the Christian axiom that nature has no reason for existence save to serve man.*

In the essay, Professor White directs his comments against Christianity. However, his real thrust is to criticize the Bible's account of creation, with its apparent "permission" to human beings to exploit the earth. If his interpretation is correct, not only Christianity, but Judaism, too, is "guilty." After all, both religious traditions consider the words of the Bible to be holy.

- **How would you interpret these verses?**

- **Have you ever understood those verses in the way White suggests, especially in his final words: *"Nature has no reason for existence save to serve man?"* If nature exists not only to serve human beings, but for other purposes, what would they be?**

- **Is White correct when he argues that our modern attitude toward the earth stems from these ancient teachings? Does this make any difference to people today, in terms of their attitudes towards the environment?**

In the years since Lynn White published his theory, many scholars in the history of religion have sought to refute him. Many base their objections on the way the Hebrew text is understood, as well as the general attitude of the Bible toward creation and the place of human beings within it. For example, James Barr, a professor at Manchester University in England, suggests [in *Bulletin of John Rylands Library*, 55:1] that the Hebrew words כְּבָשֻׁהָ and וּרְדוּ do not convey the negative associations of "conquer" and "subjugate." Rather לכבוש means "to till" or "work" the land, rather than to brutally conquer it, while לרדות means "govern," or "have dominion," without any sense of exploitation, but rather with the sense of responsibility that a leader would have for those he/she leads. Says Barr:

> *The Jewish-Christian doctrine of creation is therefore much less responsible for the ecological crisis than is suggested by arguments such as Lynn White's. On the contrary, the biblical foundation of that doctrine would tend in the opposite direction, away from a license to exploit and towards a duty to respect and protect....As far as one must speak of responsibility and guilt, I would say that the great exploitation of nature has taken place under the reign of a liberal humanism in which man no longer conceives of himself as being under a creator, and in which therefore his place of dominion in the universe and his right to dispose of nature for his own ends is, unlike the situation in the Bible, unlimited.*

These are "fighting words." In aiming at "humanism," Barr seems to be suggesting that any system of thought which places human beings and their needs and wants at the "center," which is one common way of defining *humanism*, bears greater responsibility for our current environmental predicament than either the stories or values of the Bible. As Barr sees is, the Bible emphasizes the importance of limits, especially that human beings must accept their place in God's creation, with their special, but still confined role. Such a perspective is meant to instill, he insists, a "respect" for creation, and a need to "protect" rather than exploit it.

- **Do you think that a general outlook like "humanism" really has some responsibility for our ecological crisis?**

- **In what way is this debate between White and Barr relevant to modern concerns about the environment?**

- **Do you think that the religiously observant people you know are more or less conscious of their obligations to the earth than others? Do you believe their religious tradition has shaped their attitudes? Has your Judaism influenced how you treat the earth? How?**

Yoni, as you can see, your letter has stimulated many ideas within me. Please write again soon, for I look forward to hearing your thoughts on these concerns, as well as what you discover in other letters from those Dakota Jews.

L'hitraot,

A. Gordon

GROUP ACTIVITY

- List below some Biblical stories which emphasize the limits that are to be placed on human control? For example, would you read the story of the Tower of Babel [Genesis 11] as one such illustration?

_____

_____

_____

- Read the opinions of White and Barr. Divide the room into four sections: "White," "Barr," "Neither," and "Both." Each member of the class should go to the section they agree with the most.

- Why did you choose that corner? Can you convince others to join you?

Chapter XI: Teshuvah #1

Whose world is it, anyway?

Jerusalem, Tammuz 22, 5751

Dear Yoni,

I just finished reading your recent letter, and there are so many thoughts swimming through my mind about the Tevelmanns and their predicament of how much land to cultivate. Having been to North Dakota once myself, I recall being struck by how vast it seemed. Somehow the word "plains" fits that region perfectly. They are plain, and also immense -- the vistas seem to stretch to infinity.

It's incredible to imagine that these simple Dakota Jews, desperate to make a home for themselves in a new land, should pause to consider an issue that has turned out to be central to modern environmental concerns. It might be stated this way: **Is there a value in leaving land alone, in never touching it?**

While I am familiar with the sources your great great grandfather apparently used in framing his answer, I wonder what he finally ended up saying. Did he applaud the notion of "raw" land, of wilderness? Personally, it has never seemed that Jews have been enthusiasts of the wilderness. After all, the "wilderness" experience of the people of Israel was dreadful. The Exodus story makes clear that our ancestors were "condemned" to the wilderness. Moreover, there are plenty of stories in Jewish literature from later times which paint the wilderness as a place of danger and forlorn values. Is it possible that Rabbi Schein would have extolled the idea of leaving some land uncivilized?

Then, too, I wonder how he responded to the letter's reference to Theodore Roosevelt. The truth is that those Dakota Jews might not have been completely accurate in their portrayal of him. They speak of Roosevelt's "great interest in the preservation of wilderness." On one level, that's true. He was instrumental in helping push through the legislation that created the national parks at Yosemite, Yellowstone and Mount Rainier. However, he was not so much interested in "preservation" as he was in "conservation" -- and upon the difference between those two terms hangs one of the central debates in the modern environmental movement.

Those called "preservationists" -- and a great example would be someone like John Muir, whose prodigious efforts in northern California helped save the giant redwoods -- believe that certain defined areas should be "off limits." Period! There should be no development, no harvesting, no anything. Certain areas ought to be left as they were, forever. Hence the term -- "preservationists."

Roosevelt would more accurately be defined as a "conservationist." He believed that land ought to be saved, so that it could be put to "multiple use." People like him contend that good land management can enable wilderness areas to be, on the one hand, admired and enjoyed by naturalists, but also can yield economic benefits for the good of people, such as in lumbering and mining or grazing -- so long as it is done in a responsible way.

- **Do you regard yourself as a conservationist, or as a preservationist? Both? Neither?**

In some respects, this debate between the preservationsists and the conservationsists is a superb example of a fundamental question within the ecological movement, which might be stated this way: **Is the earth here for human use, or does the earth belong to no one -- or to a power beyond?** One way of framing this debate is between two "isms." Specialists speak of the clash between **anthropocentrism vs. biocentrism**.

As the word itself implies, **anthropocentrism** means putting **human beings at the center**, that in making decisions about nature and how to use it, the primary consideration must be acting for the good of human beings. As I mentioned to you in an earlier letter, some critics contend that the Bible is the source for this anthropocentric view because of the "permission slip" given to human beings in Genesis 1:27-28 to "be fertile and increase, fill the earth and master it."

An opposing orientation is known as **biocentrism**. This theory argues that the only proper human stance is one which acknowledges that **all things in the biosphere have an equal right to live** and reach full realization, that **the universe is one complete, harmonious system** in which all the parts are interrelated and depend upon one another. We must see and treat the earth as if it were, in its totality, a living, self-contained organism, that regulates and sustains itself. Doing violence to any part of it affects the entire living whole.

Rabbi Lawrence Troster wrote an article in one of our movement's journals, *Conservative Judaism* [entitled "Created in the Image of God: Humanity and Divinity in an age of Environmentalism," Volume 44:1, Fall, 1991, pp. 14-24] in which he sought to show the relationship of biocentrism to classical Judaism. While it is a sophisticated essay, with many complicated ideas, I think you might find what he has to say not only interesting, but highly relevant to the questions that the Tevelmanns were asking Rabbi Schein. Let me summarize some of it for you.

Rabbi Troster begins by noting that most teachings on Judaism and the environment adopt what is called the "stewardship" model, which bids human beings to be responsible "stewards" or guardians of the earth. In this model, human beings are in "partnership" with God in looking after the world and its creatures. Typically this approach grants human beings the "right" to use nature so long as they do so in a responsible way. Most readings of the Jewish sources on ecology assert, or at the very least imply, an anthropocentric perspective.

The biocentric model, by contrast, offers a far different viewpoint. It argues for a relationship that might be called, not "partnership," but "part-of-ship" -- that human beings are part of the same, self-contained "ship" called EARTH. Acceptance by human beings of that status in the "ship" with every other living thing should make a profound impact on how humanity approaches all living things. Writes Rabbi Troster:

> *This morality says that we must move beyond the concept of benign utilitarian management of life on earth. If human beings are a part of [this self-enclosed universe], then we must act towards the earth with a kind of moral behavior as we would with another being/creature/ourselves....*

- **Is Rabbi Troster suggesting the Golden Rule applies equally to all living things? Do you agree?**

- **What is the implication of his last phrase, which seems like an equation that can be read as "another being=creature=ourselves?"**

- **What would it mean if we approached all forms of life according to such a morality ?**

Rabbi Troster thus not only challenges us as Jews to rethink the "stewardship" model. He goes further. He believes it vital to reconcile a biocentric view with traditional Jewish thinking. To do so requires that we see ourselves in the same way that the Bible characterizes human beings -- as created בְּצֶלֶם אֱלֹהִים -- in the image of God. As we accept the significance of being created in God's image, we understand that,

> *[H]umanity is the physical extension of God's power and presence on earth. Having characteristics of both "higher" and "lower" creatures, we are aware of our connection to*

71

God, to other living beings, and of our earthly origin and limitations as well. That consciousness provides us with the self awareness to realize our responsibilities to God and to the earth we tend....

Rabbi Troster's idea here is that human beings have "characteristics of both 'higher' and 'lower' creatures" and thus approach the earth in two ways. On the one hand, having traits of the "lower" creatures means that we must use the earth to sustain ourselves. However, we humans also possess qualities of a "higher" order, for we are the "physical extension of God's power and presence."

- **How do you relate to the idea, found first in the Genesis story, and later in Jewish literature, that human beings are created "in the image of God?" For you, does it mean what Rabbi Troster suggests -- that "humanity is the physical extension of God's power and presence?"**

- **What would it mean for our enviromental behavior if we really thought of ourselves as possessing a God-like image? Do you think we would treat the world differently if we imagined it as somehow "our" creation, given that we "are the physical extension" of the Creator?**

- **Which "side" of ourselves, the 'higher' or 'lower,' is more evident in the way we routinely deal with the environment?**

- **Do you think that a biocentric stance is practical in our world today? How would your daily life be different -- in school, at the synagogue, around your neighborhood -- if you approached the world with a biocentric orientation?**

- **Finally, what about the question which the Tevelmanns asked, applied in the setting of our modern world? If we seek to reflect God's image in our own stance toward the land, does that mean that we must leave some of it untouched -- forever? Must we be, at least on some level, preservationsists rather than conservationsists?**

Whew! I'm exhausted from writing. Here's hoping my words are clear enough. Let me know your response. Already I look forward to getting your next letter and learning what else you have discovered in your treasure trove of letters.

Shalom,

A. Gordon

GROUP ACTIVITY

- Draw a line in the middle of the room. Label one end of the line "Biocentric," and the other "Anthropocentric." Each person in the class should move to the place on the line that they think reflects their personal belief. After reviewing general feelings, how do people at various points "along the line" feel about:

  - Eating meat?

  - Eating dairy products?

  - Eating grains and vegetables?

  - Development of open spaces?

  - Other issues affecting the environment?

- Given the above discussion, which view has a more direct effect on us, in terms of coaxing us to act responsibly regarding nature? Why?

**Causing needless pain to animals is forbidden. However, who decides
what is "needless" when it comes to animals?**

Jerusalem, Elul 10, 5751

Dear Yoni,

Your letter arrived just as we are beginning our preparations for the High Holy
Days, so I hasten to write now, before *Rosh Hashanah* arrives, when the whole
country takes off the month. We have plans for hiking during *Hol Ha-Moed
Sukkot* with a guide from *Haganat HaTevah*, the Israeli organization working to
preserve the country's natural wonders.

Your discoveries about those Dakota Jews are fascinating, and the most recent
letter is especially intriguing. In fact, when I told my wife about how that
community of pioneers seemed so concerned for animal life -- from whether to
permit hunting on their land to the potential abuses of *shehitah* -- she smiled and
said:

"Aharon, that just shows you that the author of *Kohelet* [the Biblical book of
Ecclesiates] was right when he said that 'there is nothing new under the sun.'
Those Dakota Jews sound as if they are the direct ancestors of the U.S.Y.'ers back
at the congregation. You remember how the youth group debated the question
of using animals for research, and that some U.S.Y.'ers were vegetarians. Doesn't
it seem likely that many of them would have voted with those Dakota Jews to ban
sending their cattle down to Chicago for slaughter?"

"I suppose so," I answered, "but as I recall it, it was a pretty hot debate, not only
about animal research -- but about vegetarianism. Some refused to eat meat
because they thought it was healthier; others did so because of the argument that
it is wrong to consume anything high on the food chain, like meat, which requires
using valuable resources. Only a few of those U.S.Y.'ers, if I remember correctly,
were vegetarians because they felt human beings had no right to take animal life."

What about your friends, Yoni?

•   **How many are vegetarians?**

•   **What reasons do they give?**

75

If there are more people who are vegetarians than there used to be, as somehow I sense, it may be due to the impact of the "animal rights" movement. This movement claims that animals have a moral standing similar to or equal to that of human beings. This movement has challenged our conventional wisdom about animals, including our understanding of what Judaism has to say about animals. An increasing number of Jews believe our religion has something to learn from -- and to contribute to -- this discussion.

From a book which I read recently, entitled *People, Penguins and Plastic Trees: Basic Issues in Environmental Ethics* [edited by Donald VanDeVeer and Christine Pierce; Wadsworth Publishing Co., Belmont, California, 1986], I learned that there are basically four different views about the *moral* relationship of animals to human beings:

1. **ANIMALS HAVE NO MORAL STANDING.** Human beings can do what they want with animals, which are a lower form of life than human life. This is a position associated with the famous seventeenth century philosopher Rene Descartes.

2. Though they have moral interests, just like human beings, **ANIMALS COUNT LESS** than do human interests. In a conflict between the needs of humans, and those of animals, human needs should matter more. However, humans must be sensitive to the feelings and needs of animals.

3. **ANIMALS AND HUMANS ARE EQUALS** in moral standing. When humans decide what actions to take with respect to animals, they must consider the animals' interests [like pain or feelings or life] on an absolutely EQUAL basis with their own human needs. This is the view advocated by the modern American philosopher Tom Regan.

4. **ANIMALS ARE HIGHER** on the moral plane than human beings. No one may actually defend this view, but the question of what to do when everyday economic interests, like jobs for loggers, clash with the desire to protect an endangered species, such as the spotted owl, suggests that some might actually favor animal interests over those of humans.

From what you wrote in your letter, Yoni, those Dakota Jews were trying to define their position. As religious Jews, it doesn't seem they could have possibly agreed with Decartes, given the strict warnings of Judaism forbidding צַעַר בַּעֲלֵי חַיִּים -- "pain inflicted on animal life."

On the other hand, it seems equally certain that they would not have agreed with any view elevating the rights of animals *above* those of human beings. Rabbi

76

Schein must have been hinting at that when he cites a source that allows human beings to use animals if there is sufficient צוֹרֶךְ -- "need."

Yet if neither of the two extremes are acceptable, what's the right position? What did those Dakota Jews do? Where should we modern Jews take our stand? Do human interests always take precedence over animal life? Are there instances which require a balancing act between the needs and interests of both human beings and animals?

Consider the following:

- **May human beings use animals for any scientific purpose? If not, what are the limits to such experimental use?**

- **Does it matter that in animal research, one scientist is seeking a cure for stomach cancer -- while another experimenter is testing the toxicity of a new suntan oil or nail polish?**

- **May medical surgeons "harvest" a baboon heart for transplanting to a human being?**

- **Are there limitations to the educational use of animals? Should high school biology students be permitted, as is the routine practice today, to dissect frogs, when any standard anatomy book contains all the information any students would need to know?**

Our _Hug Haaretz_ group discussed these questions several months back, and we based our evening's study on an halachic essay written by Rabbi J. David Bleich, who is a preeminent representative of American Orthodoxy. He contributed a comprehensive essay entitled "Judaism and Animal Experimentation" to the book _Animal Sacrifices: Religious Perspectives on the Use of Animals in Science_, edited by Tom Regan [Philadelphia: Temple University Press, 1986]. Here is a brief section from Rabbi Bleich's summary:

> _Jewish law clearly forbids any act that causes pain or discomfort to animals unless such act is designed to satisfy a legitimate human need. There is significant authority for the position that animal pain may be sanctioned only for medical purposes, including direct therapeutic benefit, medical experimentation of potential therapeutic benefit and training medical personnel. Those who eschew these positions [and thus are less stringent about the use of animals] would not sanction painful procedures for the purpose of testing or perfecting_

cosmetics. An even larger body of authority refuses to sanction inflicting pain on animals when the desired benefit can be acquired in an alternative manner.

Rabbi Bleich notes that one 19th century scholar, Rabbi Joseph Saul Nathanson, was more restrictive than many other traditional authorities. Rabbi Nathanson says that one may disregard the prohibition against צַעַר בַּעֲלֵי חַיִּים -- "causing pain to living animals" -- only if the human benefit gained is **proportionate** to the pain inflicted on the animal. Should the potential gain for human beings, however, be of a lesser magnitude than the pain inflicted on the animal, he claims that Jewish law would forbid it.

- **What would be Rabbi Bleich's responses to the issues raised before, such as dissecting frogs in high school biology class? Or taking a vital animal organ for transplanting to a human, when such an act seems EXTREMELY EXPERIMENTAL rather than of "direct therapeutic benefit?"**

- **What do you make of Rabbi Nathanson's test of "animal pain vs. human benefit?" How can one determine any meaningful way to measure that magnitude factor?**

- **Would he forbid the sort of routine tests that are performed today on underarm deodorants, in which the deodorant is force fed through a slit in animals' throats until half of them die -- as a way of testing the toxicity of the product to humans?**

- **How do you feel about such a test, especially with the knowledge that over 20 million animals are used every year for product research in the United States alone? Do you believe anything should be done about such experiments?**

As for a non-orthodox perspective on these issues, I recently came across an anthology entitled *Judaism and Ecology*, edited by Aubrey Rose [London: Cassell Publishers, 1992]. In addition to background essays on Jewish teachings about the environment, the author sketches practical steps that could be taken to implement those teachings. An essay on animal welfare also summarizes the official position of the Conference of Liberal and Progressive Rabbis of Great Britain. Here is what those rabbis [who would correspond, in North America, to most Reform and some Conservative rabbis] have to say about treating animals -- both for research and for food:

> *Much has been written and spoken against the Jewish method of slaughter but this method is actually designed*

to minimize animal suffering. The shehitah method renders an animal unconscious in a matter of seconds and it is doubtful if pain can be registered in such a short time. If it is, it can only be momentary and is as nothing compared to the life- long suffering endured by so many farm animals in our day.

"Factory farming" is an abomination, and as the Talmud demands that animals be spared pain at all costs, the products of animal husbandry must be considered as unsuitable for Jewish consumption. The Jewish consumer should purchase free-range eggs [from hens that roam freely] rather than battery eggs [from hens raised in tight cages] and avoid buying chicken or veal which derives from "intensive" farming [in which the animals cannot roam at will]. To deprive God's creatures of sunlight, fresh air, and exercise is utterly sadistic, and it is against animal husbandry, rather than shehitah, that the efforts of animal welfare societies ought to be directed.

Criticism may be directed by Judaism against research laboratories where millions of animals are yearly tortured supposedly to advance the frontiers of science....At the very least one should distinguish between experiments intended to assist medical development and those conducted for the benefit of commerce.

- **What advice would these modern rabbis have given those Dakota Jews about hunting? And about sending the animals for slaughter to Chicago?**

- **Do you agree with these rabbis that Jews should avoid foods which are raised by intensive farming methods? Should modern day Judaism contemplate incorporating such restrictions into its understanding of kashrut?**

- **What restrictions should be developed in using animals for research that would comply with Judaism's teachings about צַעַר בַּעֲלֵי חַיִּים --"pain of living animals?"**

By the way, Yoni, my colleague, Rabbi James Lebeau, wrote a sourcebook for U.S.Y. several years back called *The Jewish Dietary Laws: Sanctify Life* [United Synagogue Youth, New York, 1983], in which he tackles the question of Kashrut and humane slaughter. From time to time, questions continue to be asked about the humaneness of she_hitah, especially over the use of hoisting and shackling before slaughter.

For now, though, these are some of the questions which have occurred to me since reading about your Dakota Jews and their rabbi. I imagine that future discoveries by you and Mrs. Saltz will be equally challenging. Do keep me up to date on your detective work. Please wish all my friends back home our hopes for a sweet and peaceful year, both there and here in Israel.

Shanah Tovah,

Aharon Gordon

GROUP ACTIVITY

- **Assign each of the positions regarding the moral standing of animals listed earlier in this chapter to a specific corner of the room. After discussing briefly why the participants chose their particular corner, do they believe that animals should be used for:**

  - **General scientific experimentation?**

  - **Commercial product safety experimentation?**

  - **Medical experimentation?**

  - **Organ transplants to humans in medical need?**

  - **Food?**

  Which corners agree with Rabbi Bleich's position? With Rose's position?

80

Chapter XIII: Teshuvah #3

**Curbing population growth is essential.
Should limitations apply to everyone?**

Jerusalem, 25 Tishrei 5752

Dear Yoni,

Your letter arrived in the middle of a late fall hot spell. Because our apartment doesn't have air conditioning, we have taken to searching out cool places to while away the scorching temperatures. Yesterday, we went to the Israel Museum.

As we sat and waited for the museum to open, I re-read your letter. It was fascinating to learn how those North Dakota Jews were struggling with the question of how many babies to have, given their limited resources. In some ways, we Israeli Jews are like them in that we, too, are very conscious of the number of children we have.

Let me give you one example, which was apparent at the museum entrance. Standing in front of us was a large family. There must have been six or seven children. When they came up to the ticket line, they were admitted at a SUPER discount. You see, the museum not only sells cheaper tickets to the elderly and all students; they admit large families for next to nothing. The ticket sign says it quite plainly: הנחות מיוחדות למשפחות מבורכות ברב בנים -- "Special deductions for families blessed abundantly with children."

That placard, it occurs to me, says a great deal. Our tradition affirms, beginning with the creation story in Genesis, that giving birth to children is one of humanity's greatest commandments, one of God's truest blessings. Genesis 1:28 declares quite emphatically: פְּרוּ וּרְבוּ וּמִלְאוּ אֶת הָאָרֶץ -- "Be FRUITFUL and MULTIPLY and FILL the LAND.

I suspect that the concern of Israeli Jews about the number of Jews in the world has as much to do with the specifics of that command as it does with the reality of what has happened -- and is happening -- to the number of Jews in our world, from the devastations of the Holocaust, to the forced assimilation of Jews in the former Soviet Union, to the deep concerns about the future of all Jews who live in an open society and therefore run the risks of intermarriage.

Those of us Israelis who are environmentally conscious realize that we are caught on the horns of a dilemma. On the one hand, we really do agree with the need for Jews to replenish our thin ranks. That has a special urgency here in Israel, too, where Jews think a great deal about the high birth rate of the Arab population and whether one day it will outnumber the Jewish populace. On the other hand, we must face squarely one of the great problems ecology experts address: **Can the planet support a monumentally ever-increasing human population?**

As you probably know, since you are studying the subject, the figures are staggering. World population is growing at about 2% a year. That may not seem like a lot, but it's a huge number, because it compounds quickly. Here's one example: recently, the United Nations estimated that 235,000 *additional* people were being born *each day.* Multiply that figure by 365, add the 2% increase, and it seems quite clear that we human beings are reproducing at numbers that only can be called astronomical.

This is hardly a new problem. Writing in 1798, a British political economist, Thomas Malthus, had warned that human beings were having far more progeny than the world could possibly feed. He predicted that eventually, many would face starvation. However, technology -- like more efficient equipment, better seed, greater control of disease and pests -- proved Malthus wrong. He also did not anticipate the success of birth control in stemming the growth of population.

Today, however, the debate over Malthus' predictions has been renewed. Perhaps the most famous modern advocate of his views is the famous biologist Paul Ehrlich. He wrote a bestseller, *The Population Bomb,* in which he put forth the view that the growth of population, especially in the developing countries, was certain to have a disastrous impact on the environment, even after taking into account the technological revolutions of the 20th century. Uncontrolled population, he argued, not only would deplete the earth's finite resources. The numbers, and especially the density, would inevitably lead to urban decay and the spread of disease.

Many environmentalists do not agree with Ehrlich's dire prophecies. They argue that the question is not the number of people -- but the way our resources of land and water and fertilizer are used. But they insist that if we conclude that the real question is not how many babies are born -- but how we will ourselves to take care of all those fresh lives -- it will still require tremendous effort. We shall, they say, have to rethink how we produce food, and especially how we consume it, so that we can ecologically take care of this planet that must house ever more people in the decades and centuries ahead. These debates are particularly fascinating from a religious perspective, given the clear emphasis in the Bible on the blessing of procreation.

These are just some of the questions which place the issues of *population stabilization* on the agenda of ecologically-minded Jews. Though not all that many Jewish thinkers have addressed these questions directly, two highly regarded American rabbis have. Here are brief excerpts from their writings.

The first is by Robert Gordis, a distinguished Conservative rabbi who not only held a congregational pulpit but taught at the Jewish Theological Seminary and wrote scholarly books on many subjects, from Bible to Jewish theology. His article is entitled "Birth Control, Group Survival and the Population Explosion," from his book *Love & Sex -- A Modern Jewish Perspective* [New York: Farrar Straus Giroux, 1978]:

> *Modern Judaism unequivocally reaffirms the obligation to perpetuate the human race through the medium of the family as a basic and general goal. But it recognizes also that family planning is often a necessity of modern life, in view of complex moral, hygienic and economic factors.*
>
> *Failure to employ birth control in the face of the menace of the population explosion may well represent the final transgression in the long catalogue of sins that will bring the human race to the brink of extinction.*
>
> *On a smaller scale, but equally perilous, is the opposite threat facing the Jewish people -- not overpopulation but genocide from within and without.*
>
> *There is no real contradiction between urging the practice of birth control upon many nations in Asia, Africa and South America, in order to meet the menace of overpopulation -- and calling for larger families in the Jewish community. Birth control is not an end in itself. When it serves to advance human welfare, as is the case of the underdeveloped beset with overcrowding, grinding poverty, disease and lack of economic resources, the practice of family limitation is a necessity. Where families have become too small even to reproduce themselves, as is the case in the Jewish community, birth control should be used sparingly and only when warranted.*

- **How do you respond to the distinction Gordis draws between what should be done in developing countries -- and within the Jewish community?**

- **Is this position discriminatory, urging population control for certain peoples but not for Jews?**

A second excerpt is from an essay by Moses Tendler, a foremost spokesman for Orthodox Judaism in this country. At Yeshiva University in New York City, he was professor of Talmud and chair of the Biology department. The essay is called "Population Control -- The Jewish View," in *Jewish Bioethics*, edited by Fred Rosner and J. David Bleich [New York: Sanhedrin Press, 1979]:

> Inherent in our concept of a personal God is the philosophy of the verse in Psalm 145 [the Ashrei] in which God provides sustenance for all His creatures פּוֹתֵחַ אֶת יָדֶךָ וּמַשְׂבִּיעַ לְכָל חַי רָצוֹן. -- "God opens His hands and sustains all life." Food supply and world population are areas of divine concern.

> The management of the world's population is relegated unto God. However man has been granted a junior partnership in the management of this world. Man is permitted, even required, to use his partnership rights to regulate his own affairs, on condition that he does not violate the by-laws of this God-man relationship that are formulated in the Torah.

> The Jew as a world citizen is personally concerned with famine in India and China. Before a Jew can support birth control clinics in overpopulated areas of the world, he must insist that there be heroic efforts made to utilize fully the agricultural potential of the world.

> There are different guidelines for the Jew on this question. If reduction in the birthrate of the famine-threatened population of the world is indeed the proper response, then the Jews as world citizens should join in the world-wide effort of providing contraceptive materials to those desirous of limiting family size. The Jew, as a Jew, must at the same time reject the suggestion that he, too, must limit the size of his family. We have unique problems created for us by world citizenry. Six and one half million Jews destroyed at the hands of world citizenry in one generation represents a staggering loss.

- **How do you interpret Tendler's faith assertion that God has ultimate responsibility to assure that there will be enough food for all life?**

84

- What can Rabbi Tendler mean when he says that the "management of the world's population is relegated unto God?" Do you accept that as true?

- Are we to assume that our world can sustain ALL human life born within it?

- What about the environmental ramifications of NOT interfering in population growth -- which must inevitably lead to clearing more and more land, and/or relying on even more potentially harmful means of production, like chemical fertilizers and pesticides?

- What does it mean that human beings have a "junior partnership" in caring for the earth? How do we as Jews reconcile the need for "caring for the earth" with the command to be "fruitful and multiply" when those two obligations seem now in conflict?

- Would you defend Tendler's "different guidelines" for Jews? How?

These questions are some of the more perplexing ones we have been struggling with in our own discussions at *Hug Haaretz*. I would welcome your views -- especially about how Rabbi Schein might have responded to these modern dilemmas of population.

Please write when you have a chance, which I hope is soon. I do hope that you had as wonderful a *Sukkot* and *Simhat Torah* as we had here. I recall with fondness the fabulous autumn colors which made the fall *hagim* [festivals] so special back home.

B'vrachah,

Aharon G.

GROUP ACTIVITY

- Debate the following resolution: "Resolved: That Jews should actively encourage use of birth control in order to reign in population growth."

Chapter XIV: Teshuvah #4

Sometimes nature's demands can challenge our observance of *Shabbat*. However, *Shabbat* can also teach us to respect nature.

Jerusalem, Adar Bet 25, 5752

Dear Yoni,

It has been nearly three months since last we were in touch, and I was growing concerned when I didn't hear from you. Now I understand the cause for the delay.

We are so sad to hear of Mrs. Saltz's death. She was, as you discovered, an extraordinary woman. In many ways, she was far, far ahead of her time. One day, soon after I had come to the congregation, I found her studying a page of Talmud in the shul library. "Can you really make your way through that?" I asked naively. "Of course, I can," she responded. "Probably better than some of those first year rabbinical students."

Her response seemed to contain just a trace of bitterness. Actually it was more like sorrow, and eventually I came to understand why. Mrs. Saltz had wanted to be a rabbi. Her father actually encouraged her. Times being what they were then, she stood no chance of being admitted, much less graduating. Eventually she gave up that dream, married and moved out to the Twin Cities, where, as you know, she led a wonderful, active life. All of us who knew her well recognized her brightness, felt her passion and identified with her love of Judaism.

I am so grateful that your discovery of the Tevelmann letters led you to her, for that enabled yet another generation to be shaped by her. I pray that her memory will bless your life, and it has ours.

Since your letter not only carried the news of Mrs. Saltz's death, but also contained a copy of one of the letters she translated with you, I do want to take a moment to react to it. By coincidence, the mail reached us after *Purim* and our annual trek away from Jerusalem. Because we don't use the car on *Shabbat* and the *Hagim*, holidays like *Purim*, when everyone is on *hofesh* [vacation], are one of the few times we motor around the country. It was good timing because something which happened on our vacation helps me better understand the predicament related by the Tevelmanns.

This past holiday, we traveled to visit good friends who made *aliyah* to *kibbutz*. It was a wonderful visit. The highlight, though this might sound hard to believe, was working side by side with my friend in the *refet* -- the cowshed. We spent a couple of hours assisting the regular <u>haverim</u> in milking their huge herd. Being a city slicker, I rarely get a chance to engage in such earthy (and trust me, it was *very earthy*) work.

In the course of the shift, I asked my friend about the *halachah* of *Shabbat*. Didn't they have to milk the cows everyday, including *Shabbat*? Did they use the electric equipment? How could they do that, and still pass muster with the Israeli orthodox rabbinate? My friend answered by telling me that my questions were exactly the sort that were asked by the first religious pioneers in the country 50 years ago. After they established their first *kibbutzim*, those early *chalutzim* faced the puzzle of reconciling what Nature demanded against what *Shabbat* forbade: the strenuous work of milking the cows.

As it turns out, when those *kibbutzniks* turned to the chief rabbi for a solution to this conflict, his response confounded them. The rabbi told them to hire gentiles to do the work. My friend said that the *kibbutzniks* balked at having someone else do what they believed was rightfully their own responsibility. Ultimately, they found their way out of their dilemma when automatic milking equipment was developed, which could be set on special *Shabbat* timers so that the machines turned on and off by themselves. That invention enabled religious *kibbutzim* to raise cows, respect the demands of nature, and observe the requirements for *Shabbat* -- all at the same time. Their dilemma, it seems to me, is not unlike the one you wrote about in your most recent letter. Then, too, those Dakota Jews needed to reconcile their observance of *halachah* and what might be demanded of them in the fields at harvest time.

Such conflicts between the commands of *Shabbat* and the needs of nature are especially significant to us religiously observant Israelis who are environmentally attuned. You see, we routinely look to the *Shabbat* as a primary inspiration of how to properly treat nature. Let me give you a simple but powerful example of how we make that connection.

On one of our first *Shabbat*ot after making *aliyah*, my wife and I went for a walk. I commented that something in the air seemed different, but I couldn't figure it out. Then it occurred to us. The air smelled cleaner. And for a simple reason. *It was!* Israeli automobiles and buses use a lot of diesel fuel, and during the week, the air often reeks from the smell of spent fuel. But on *Shabbat*, when there is no public transportation, and many fewer private cars ply the road, there is a noticeable improvement in the air quality.

That awareness was, for me, a potent recognition of the way *Shabbat* observance can enlighten us about the environment. What would it be like, I wondered, if we could let go of our automobiles and buses -- just a little bit? Wouldn't the world be a cleaner, if not a better, place? That's what that *Shabbat* moment seemed to be saying to me. What's interesting is the way two illustrious 20th century Jews -- one quite *un*traditional, the other very traditional -- recognized this intrinsic connection between Jewish observance and our world -- long before anyone could have imagined our current environmental problems. Here are two brief excerpts from their writings.

The first is from Erich Fromm [1900-1980], a famed psychoanalyst, who wrote about the symbolic significance of *Shabbat* in two of his works -- *The Forgotten Language* [New York: Holt Rinehart and Winston, 1951] and *You Shall Be As Gods* [New York: Holt Rinehart and Winston, 1966]. This section below is from the second book, which begins by raising a set of questions: Why are there so many work restrictions associated with *Shabbat*? And not just about work in the ordinary sense of activities which demand physical exertion -- but even seemingly innocent, innocuous activities, notes Fromm, like "pulling a single blade of grass from the soil; carrying anything; even something as light as carrying a handkerchief on one's person." He answers his own questions this way:

> *The concept of work underlying the biblical and later Talmudic concepts is not one of physical effort, but it can be defined thus: 'Work' is any interference by man, be it constructive or destructive, with the physical world. 'Rest' is a state of peace between man and nature. Man must leave nature untouched, not change it in any way, either by building or by destroying anything. Even the smallest change made by man in the natural process is a violation of rest.*
>
> *On the basis of the general definition, we can understand the Sabbath ritual. Any heavy work, like plowing or building, is work in this, as well as in our modern, sense. But lighting a match and pulling up a blade of grass, while not requiring any effort, are symbols of human interference with the natural process, are a breach of peace between man and nature.*
>
> *On the basis of this principle, we can understand the Talmudic prohibition of carrying anything, even of little weight, on one's person....I must not carry even a handkerchief from one domain to another -- for instance, from the private domain of the house to the public domain*

of the street. This law is a natural extension of the idea of peace from the social to the natural realm. A man must not interfere with or change the natural equilibrium and he must refrain from changing the social equilibrium. That means not only not to do business but to avoid the most primitive from of transference of property, namely, its local transference from one domain to another.

The Sabbath symbolizes a state of union between man and nature and between man and man. By not working -- that is say, by not participating in the process of natural change -- man is free from the chains of time, although only for one day a week.

- **Fromm speaks of work as a "breach of peace", but *Shabbat* as "a state of union" between human beings and nature. Do you agree with those characterizations?**

- **Try describing what it would mean to be in such a "state of union."**

- **Can observing the one day of *Shabbat* in a symbolic "state of union" make any difference in how we treat the environment the rest of the week?**

A second selection comes from the writings of my former teacher at the Jewish Theological Seminary, Professor Abraham Joshua Heschel [1907-1972]. Probably his most famous book was *The Sabbath* [New York: Harper Torchbooks, 1966], first published in 1951, the same year as Fromm's. Here is the way Professor Heschel speaks of the connection between *Shabbat* and our concern for the world:

To set apart one day a week for freedom, a day on which we would not use the instruments which have been so easily turned into weapons of destruction, a day for being with ourselves, a day of detachment from the vulgar, of independence from external obligation, a day on which we stop worshipping the idols of technical civilization, a day on which we use no money, a day of armistice in the economic struggle with our fellow men and the forces of nature -- is there any institution that holds out a greater hope for man's progress than the Sabbath?

The solution of mankind's most vexing problem will not be found in renouncing technical civilization, but in attaining some degree of independence of it.

In regard to external gifts, to outward possessions, there is only one proper attitude -- to have them and to be able to do without them. On the Sabbath we live, as it were, independent of technical civilization: we abstain primarily from any activity that aims at remaking or reshaping the things of space. Man's royal privilege to conquer nature is suspended on the seventh day.

- **What is so beguiling about technology that Heschel must warn of its power?**

- **What does Heschel mean by "royal privilege to conquer nature?"**

- **Can a weekly suspension of that privilege make any difference? How?**

Yoni -- I must close for now, so that I can take this letter to the post office before it closes for *Shabbat*. Please write again soon -- and a joyous *Pesah* to all of you. Most of all, we hope that time continues to lighten the sadness of Mrs. Saltz's death and that you are strengthened by your remembrances of her.

Hag Kasher v'Sameah

Aharon G.

GROUP ACTIVITY

- **List below ways you and/or your family change their behavior on *Shabbat*:**

1. _____

2. _____

3. _____

4. _____

5. _____

6. _____

7. _____

8. _____

- **How many of these conserve a natural resource? How many involve Heschel's idea of removing ourselves from "technical civilization?" Are there additional things you could do that can enhance these two principles in your *Shabbat* observance?**

Chapter XV

Yoni attends *Shabbat* services

Red lights going one way, white lights going the other. But this time we were in the middle of it. We were on our way to my synagogue before *Shabbat*, fighting the tail-end of rush hour traffic to make it to the synagogue in time for Friday evening services.

A steady line of cars sifted out of the stream of traffic and into the synagogue parking lot. As we waited in line it occurred to me that the smell of exhaust hadn't lessened now that we were no longer on the highway. If anything, being in the slow moving line of cars made the smell worse.

On the far side of the lot, the synagogue sparkled with bright light. Flood lights shone up at the front of the building. The series of large windows around the sanctuary were aglow as well, white light shining through some of them, deep reds through the others. Cars honked to signal friends of their passengers' arrival, and then continued grinding their way across the gravel; a herd of metal dinosaurs, settling into their den.

As we made our way across the lot, my thoughts were stuck on Rabbi Gordon's description of *Shabbat* in Jerusalem. A *Shabbat* free of the smells and sounds, the rush and crush of cars and buses. By the time we came to "*ha-Pores Sukkat Shalom Aleinu, v'al col amo Yisrael, v'al Yerushalayim,*" [who extends his shelter of peace upon us, upon all the people of Israel, and upon Jerusalem], I was completely taken up with a vision of *Shabbat* without cars. During *Magen Avot*, which is normally one of my favorite parts of the Friday evening service, I constructed the following chart in my head:

	Electricity	Cars	Buses	Paper
Sunday				
Monday				
Tuesday				
Wednesday				
Thursday				
Friday				
Shabbat				

My plan was to keep track of how much paper and electricity I used and how many miles I rode in a car or bus each week. I figured that one seventh of that total would give me an idea of the "environmental savings" that would result from not using cars and electrical devices on *Shabbat*. I realized my method might not be perfect--but I'd get a rough idea.

I managed to keep the chart for twelve days. It turned out that I averaged about sixty miles of private car use per week, and rode the school bus for another sixty. I had some sort of electrical device running during about forty percent of my waking hours -- mostly the TV, CD player and computer -- but also the microwave, toaster oven, radio, clothes dryer, etc. And I used a lot of paper -- computer paper, toilet paper, newspaper, notebook paper....

I didn't know how to translate these figures into pounds of carbon dioxide produced or kilowatts used, but for me the critical point was that I was consuming most of it unconsciously. I was using all this stuff each week and leaving behind more waste than most people in the world do in a month, or a year.

The *parshiot* [weekly portions of the Torah] for the two weeks I kept the chart were *Bo* and *va'Era*, which are taken up, for the most part, with describing the plagues God brought upon Egypt. Those *parshiyot* must have been on my mind as I added up the totals from my chart because when I had finished a strange thought came to mind: We are the locusts, I thought, and we are Egypt....

GROUP ACTIVITY

- We've talked about the need to cut wasteful practices from several different perspectives: *Bal Tash'hit* (prohibiting wanton destruction), a sense of stewardship for our world, our unity with the world, the inspiration *Shabbat* gives us to allow the world to rest as well, etc.

  Using the chart below, construct ways you will change your behavior, in order to consume fewer resources every day. Share your ideas with others:

  RESOURCE   **WHAT CAN YOU DO TO CONSERVE?**

  1. _____

  2. _____

  3. _____

  4. _____

  5. _____

  6. _____

  7. _____

  8. _____

**Damage caused by smoke is forbidden; noise is a real pollutant.
Not violating our "boundaries" is required. Who defines boundaries?**

Jerusalem, Nisan 28, 5752

Dear Yoni,

It was good to receive your news-filled letter, and to catch up on all the news of your family. Please send them our warmest regards.

Reading your latest discovery about the Tevelmanns and Rabbi Schein was enthralling. As I wrote you some months back, there is a surprisingly modern tone to the inquires of those North Dakota Jews. That is especially so in their questions about the thresher -- and the effects of the smoke and ashes which it spewed all over the Freidmans' land. I had always thought that the quality of our air -- and what we are doing to it with the pollutants from our technological lifestyle -- are issues unique to our generation. That those farmers were worried about it came as a welcome surprise.

Yet their concerns seem minor by comparison to what is happening today. Moreover, it has always seemed that the issues of air quality, while among our most serious environmental challenges, are also the most difficult to get one's arms around. That's because the issues appear so subtle. Questions about air pollution, after all, are often couched in terms of "macro," or worldwide problems, like acid rain, or global warming. Yet those very real, potentially life annihilating threats seem so far removed from the everyday reality of the air outside our windows. To many, it must seem that all the talk about a crisis in our air quality is just that -- so much talk.

To be sure, back home where you live in Minneapolis, the air seems pretty good. But travel to Los Angeles in the middle of a smog alert. Or take a trip to Mexico City, with the worst air in the world. Or visit almost any country in Eastern Europe, where the sky in places like Poland, Czechoslovakia and the former Soviet Union is so filled with contaminants [called particulates in ecology circles] that schools are required to take their children *underground* into deep mines whenever gases and other pollution build up to truly dangerous levels.

It's more than that, though. There's no way to build a wall and stop the pollution of Eastern Europe from spilling over and contaminating other regions. That's where those "macro" issues come into play. Pollutants from smoke stacks in one place cause tree tops and field crops two hundred miles away to be tinged with acid. Our unrestricted use of fossil fuels threatens the upper reaches of the atmosphere, so that our everyday vocabulary is sprinkled with words like ozone depletion and the greenhouse effect. And if I remember correctly, even smog free, lake clear locales like Minneapolis are not totally free of questions about air quality. For instance, I recall, right before we left there to come on *aliyah*, the city council and citizenry were locked in a frenzied argument over the airport's impact on city life -- from the fearsome noise made by the airplanes roaring over the most beautiful neighborhoods, to the inevitable spewing of jet fuel that plagues every airport. The council was also debating whether to ban cigarette smoking in all public places. So no place, not even a beautiful Midwestern city, can ignore what is happening to our common source of life -- the air we breathe.

It is increasingly clear to me that Israelis are awakening to that truth. Just recently, the government officially announced that the next two years are to be devoted to ecological awareness -- in the schools and the media, with the hope of making an impact on how industry, as well as the common citizen, can make a difference. Perhaps, in a future letter, I can fill you in on what is happening with this initiative.

In preparation, our <u>Hug Haaretz</u> group has been studying a new book, the first comprehensive work on ecology and the Jewish tradition to be published in Hebrew. It is called אכות הסביבה במקורות היהדות -- *Environmental Quality in the Jewish Sources,* [edited by Rabbi Meir Zeichel, for the Office of Environmental Protection, Interior Department, Jerusalem, Israel, 1990]. It covers an entire range of current concerns, from water and air pollution to urban planning. In each chapter, the authors - all traditional rabbis - examine the classical rabbinic sources, from the Talmud through the responsa literature.

Many of the sources cited are identical to those your great great grandfather apparently used in writing to the Tevelmanns and their co-workers. That coincidence has led me to wonder if he would have also agreed with these modern rabbis in their assessment of the overriding basic principles of ecological awareness in Judaism. Here is what they say:

> *Most environmental damages are considered* גרמא *--*
> *garma [the Talmudic word for damages which arise in an*
> *indirect action]. This type of damage is NOT specifically*
> *enumerated in the Torah. Rather, this concept of*
> *responsibility for one having caused indirect damages*
> *can be based, according to the* Rishonim *[those medieval*
> *sages living from the 11th to 15th centuries] on several*
> *verses in the Torah. Some ground their reasoning on the*

98

passage [from Kedoshim, Leviticus 19:18], "And you shall love your neighbor as yourself." Others assert that the proper verse to justify such injuries is [Leviticus 19:12], "and you shall not put a stumbling block before the blind." Still other rabbis maintain that the true basis for these laws is a passage from Proverbs [3:17], "its [the Torah's] paths are paths of pleasantness, and all its by-ways lead to Shalom."

- **Responsibility for indirect damages was of real consequence in Jewish law. Do you think it reasonable to ground such potentially serious consequences as monetary fines on the verse, "And you shall love your neighbor as yourself?"**

- **How does the verse "And you shall not put a stumbling block before the blind" serve as a support for assigning responsibility in this instance?**

- **What about the citation from the Book of Proverbs? In what way does it substantiate the legal concept of גרמא -- *garma* [indirect responsibility]?**

- **Can you think of other verses in Torah which can serve as the basis for such laws?**

I must tell you, Yoni, that if I were searching for a verse from Torah around which to build ecological awareness on the questions raised by the Tevelmanns, I might look, not only to the verses cited above, but at one other. It is a command found in Deuteronomy 19:14, where it says:

"You shall not move your neighbor's landmarks, set up by previous generations, in the property that will be allotted to you in the Land that the Lord your God is giving you to possess."

לֹא תַסִּיג גְּבוּל רֵעֲךָ אֲשֶׁר גָּבְלוּ רִאשֹׁנִים בְּנַחֲלָתְךָ אֲשֶׁר תִּנְחַל בָּאָרֶץ אֲשֶׁר ה־ אֱלֹקֶיךָ נֹתֵן לְךָ לְרִשְׁתָּהּ.

Originally, the verse had specific reference to the physical land of Israel, and was a clear admonition to individuals to respect the *property* rights of their neighbors.

Over time, though, this verse took on a life of its own in the Jewish legal tradition. In fact, an entire body of Jewish law is based on the verse, called the laws of הסגת גבול -- *hassagat gevul*. The meanings of property rights and landmarks were increasingly expanded, so that the verse has been seen as a warning against appropriating, not only real property, but also other "valuables" too. For example, this verse has been used by the codes [encyclopedias of Jewish law written in the Middle Ages] to justify punishing those who steal someone's legitimate right to practice a business in a given location, or who abscond with someone's intellectual property, be it an idea, artistic creation or religious teaching.

The codes also developed a category of law that reflected the importance of neighbors respecting each other's property. I can only guess that Rabbi Schein was very familiar with this category, which is called *Hilchot Shechaynim* -- The Laws of Neighbors. Here are two excerpts from the Code of Maimonides that raise interesting implications for our responsibility for the purity of the air:

6:12 --- If there is a shop in a courtyard the neighbors can protest, saying: "We cannot sleep because of the noise coming and going." The owner of the shop may, however, do his work in his shop, but he must sell only in the market. In that case, they cannot protest: "We cannot sleep because of the noise of the hammer or of the mill," since he has already established his right to have a workshop."

חֲנוּת שֶׁבֶּחָצֵר יְכוֹלִין הַשְּׁכֵנִים לִמְחוֹת בְּיָדוֹ וְלוֹמַר לוֹ: אֵין אָנוּ יְכוֹלִין לִישָׁן מִקּוֹל הַנִּכְנָסִים וְהַיּוֹצִין, אֶלָּא עוֹשֶׂה מְלַאכְתּוֹ בַּחֲנוּתוֹ וּמוֹכֵר בַּשּׁוּק, אֲבָל אֵינָם יְכוֹלִין לִמְחוֹת בְּיָדוֹ וְלוֹמַר לוֹ: אֵין אָנוּ יְכוֹלִין לִישָׁן מִקּוֹל הַפַּטִּישׁ אוֹ מִקּוֹל הָרֵחַיִם, שֶׁהֲרֵי הֶחֱזִיק לַעֲשׂוֹת כֵּן.

10:5 To what can this [the damage done by one individual to a neighbor's property or person] be compared? To one who stands on his property and shoots arrows into his fellow's courtyard and claims: "I am doing it on my premises." In such an instance, we have a right to hinder him from doing so.

הָא לְמָה זֶה דּוֹמֶה? לְמִי שֶׁעוֹמֵד בִּרְשׁוּתוֹ וְיוֹרֶה חִצִּים לַחֲצַר חֲבֵרוֹ וְאָמַר: בִּרְשׁוּתִי אֲנִי עוֹשֶׂה -- שְׁמוֹנְעִין אוֹתוֹ.

- **In the first excerpt, what is the basis for the distinction drawn between legitimate and non-legitimate rights of protest? Do you agree with the distinction? How might this distinction apply to air or noise pollution?**

- **Some rabbis use the second excerpt as the basis for banning "second hand" cigarette smoke or industrial pollution. Is doing so too far a "stretch" of what Maimonides was teaching?**

The second excerpt reminds me of a famous midrash found in *Vayikra Rabbah* [4:6], in which a rabbi offers a parable about individual actions and their impact on the community at large:

Taught Rabbi Shimon ben Yohai: How can we best understand this? As a group of people sitting in a boat. One of them takes a drill and begins making a hole beneath his seat. His companions say to him: "What are you sitting and doing?" He said to them: "What do you care? Am I not drilling beneath my own seat?" They answered: "But the waters will rise and drown all of us!"

תָּנֵי ר׳ שִׁמְעוֹן בֶּן יוֹחַאי: מָשָׁל לִבְנֵי אָדָם שֶׁהָיוּ יוֹשְׁבִין בַּסְּפִינָה, נָטַל אֶחָד מֵהֶן מַקְדֵחַ וְהִתְחִיל קוֹדֵחַ תַּחְתָּיו, אָמְרוּ לוֹ חֲבֵרָיו: מָה אַתָּה יוֹשֵׁב וְעוֹשֶׂה?! אָמַר לָהֶם: מָה אִכְפַּת לָכֶם, לֹא תַחְתַּי אֲנִי קוֹדֵחַ?! אָמְרוּ לוֹ: שֶׁהַמַּיִם עוֹלִין וּמְצִיפִין עָלֵינוּ אֶת הַסְּפִינָה!

For me, this rabbinic story sums up my anxieties about so much of our environmental crisis. As some ecologists tell us, our earth might best be likened to one BIG SHIP. If someone -- or some industry or nation or person -- decides to cavalierly do what they will with their "little piece" of that SHIP we call "the universe," there is a real possibility that all creation will drown. That's among the most powerful reasons my friends and I study the environment, and debate what are our responsibilities to it. So it is not just, as Maimonides tells us, about someone shooting arrows into someone else's space. What we do to the environment seems also about shooting arrows **into our own living space**.

In some ways, those Dakota Jews must have sensed likewise, which must explain their letter to Rabbi Schein. I look forward to hearing what else you discover they had to say -- not only about being good neighbors in their settlement, but also good citizens of the world.

Shalom, Aharon G.

GROUP ACTIVITY

- **List below some things you do in your own "space," which have an impact on other people:**

_____

_____

_____

Is *Shabbat* Enough?

Jerusalem, 4 Sivan 5752

Dear Yoni,

Lurching along in the Egged city bus through Jerusalem's ever increasingly clogged streets made it a trying venture to read your most latest letter about the Tevelmanns. What a dilemma they seemed to face -- perhaps the most formidable of all for them! And their way of formulating that challenge seems especially heartfelt -- "Are there limits to human need? Is enough ever really enough?"

After I shared this letter with my *Hug Haaretz* group, we plunged into how we Israelis might answer those questions. Not unlike those Dakota Jews, we too have lived through pioneering days, in which it took all our energy and resources just to scrape by. Those days are over in Israel. In many ways, we are very, very middle class. Automobiles everywhere, TV's and VCR's and microwaves, larger and larger apartments and homes -- the list goes on and on. Now another technological revolution has reached Jerusalem -- cable TV.

To some of my friends in the group, the arrival of multiple channels and advertising galore on cable television represents but the latest obstacle to helping Israel become more environmentally sensitive. That's because, they argue, the world of TV advertisement pushes us Israelis in just the wrong direction from where we ought to be headed -- and just at the wrong time.

The government, as I believe I mentioned in an earlier letter, has just announced that the coming two years are to be devoted to making Israel's environment better. How can we possibly hope to change how much we consume and waste, my friends ask, when the TV keeps after us with all its messages, some blatant, others subtle, about "needing that and wanting this." Instead of curbing our consumer appetite, the TV now bombards us with messages about larger/newer/faster cars, or bigger/better furniture. It is precisely the opposite message from the one we environmentalists want to convey -- that **we can do with less**, that **we must do with less** of everything if we are not to deplete the world's resources? How can Israelis possibly learn to do with "less" in our newly discovered TV age of "more?"

What's especially interesting about all this is that the early opponents of bringing television to Israel anticipated this would happen. David ben Gurion, the country's first Prime Minister, fought incessantly against the idea of introducing television into the country. He was convinced that once here, TV programming and its never ending commercials would have a corrupting influence on the nation, pushing the Israelis to rampant consumerism.

Perhaps Ben Gurion was right! Maybe my friends in the _Hug Haaretz_ group are right, too, when they aim their criticism at TV. Yet, I rather think that the issue of how much we consume, and whether we can learn to live with less, is a more personal issue, one that each of us has to take responsibility for ourselves, rather than blaming the media or the general culture.

I also believe that Judaism has something very important to teach us about learning to live with less. A superb perspective on this is to be found in an essay that Dr. Ismar Schorsch, the Chancellor of our Jewish Theological Seminary, wrote. His article appears in _Spirit and Nature: Why the Environment is a Religious Issue_ [edited by Steven C. Rockefeller and John C. Elder, Boston: Beacon Press, 1992]. I have selected three brief sections which I think you might find of interest:

> _The product largely of an agrarian society, halachah, a word that connotes "boundary," is filled with regulations designed to rein in man's unlimited use of his environment. What is consistently deemed acceptable is far short of what is within human reach. The answer to the vexing question of "how much is enough" is not determined solely by commercial interests._

- **Is there any "ecological" significance that the word halachah comes from a word for "boundary?"**

- **Is one solution to our environmental problems to be found in the creation of special halachot?**

- **In countries like the U.S. and Canada, does that mean that environmentalists ought to lobby for more and more regulations? Do such regulations really do good in changing our personal behavior?**

> _The use of land is restricted by religious values of some consequence. Perhaps best known is the institution of the sabbatical year in which the land was to lie fallow [left unplanted] and whatever grew naturally was to be shared by man and beast. But the Bible also enjoins_

against harvesting the corners of your field or returning for gleanings -- both to be left to the indigent without offense to their dignity. Crops were not to be mixed within the same field nor animals of different species interbred, an apparent expression of respect for the divine ordering of animate things. In fact, God was perceived to be an active partner in the production of all life, and hence first fruits and offspring, even human, belonged to God.... Even the bearing of children, hardly unrelated to our demands on the land, is guided by the same spirit of moderate restraint.

• **According to the Bible, living by the human/Divine partnership meant that the first fruits of the field and the flocks were given to the Temple and the *Cohanim/Leviim*. First born children also belonged to God, but through the ritual of *pidyon haben*, were redeemed. What would it mean today for us to be in partnership with God? Where should we give our "first fruits" as a sign of that partnership?**

• **Dr. Schorsch comments about "moderate restraint" in the bearing of children. What does that mean for the Tevelmanns' questions about how many babies to have, and our corresponding discussion about population stabilization and the unique aspects of our relatively tiny worldwide Jewish population?**

Lastly, an unmistakable strain of self-denial runs through the Jewish calendar. From the sacrificial cult of the temple to the synagogue of rabbinic Judaism, it is the absolute cessation of work that distinguishes celebration of Jewish holy days. Whether it be the annual harvest festival of Passover, Shavuot or Succot or the weekly Sabbath day, spiritual renewal is effected through physical contraction.... The regimen of rest is meant to restrict our strength as much as to restore it, to deflate our arrogance as much as to ennoble our spirit. The final intent of the opening chapter of Genesis is to pave the way for limits. It anchors the later and unnatural command to rest weekly in a cosmic act and induces us to acknowledge in deed, not word, that our dominion is partial. To spend one-seventh of one's life in "unproductive" rest is scarcely a mark of absolute power.

- Like Fromm and Heschel, Schorsch points to *Shabbat*, and its message of restraint and liberation from "things" and "productivity," as a potent teacher about how modern persons should treat the world and its resources. But given the state of the environment today, is it enough just to use one-seventh less?

- How is "spiritual renewal" effected "through "physical contraction?" What is the relationship of such "physical contraction" to our environmental renewal of creation?

- How can human beings best participate in the "physical renewal" of the universe, which is a responsibility we share with God, and which we read about each day in the morning service, when we say: "In Your goodness, day after day You renew creation."

Yoni -- I look forward to your response, and to that of your generation.

B'shefa berachot,

Aharon G.

GROUP ACTIVITY

- Erich Fromm, Abraham Heschel, and now Ismar Schorsch each assert that the Biblical message is one of restraint, not license, and that a basic message in the first chapter of Genesis is about the need to curb human appetites to dominate the world, rather than about giving human beings ultimate power to use the natural world.

    How should this make a difference in everyday Jewish life. How does your synagogue, and your Jewish community, reflect this perspective of "self restraint?" Does your household? In which ways? If not, how might change be made?

    List your ideas below:

    _____

    _____

    _____

    _____

אתמול, בפינה נשכחת של מחסן הקיבוץ שלנו, על יד ערמה מאובקת של קשואים מחגיגת יום האצמאות של מדינת ישראל המֵאָי שלנו, מצאתי ארגז. כבר הייתי במחסן פעמים רבות, אבל עד אתמול לא שמתי לב לארגז. לפחות לא עלה על דעתי לפתוח אותו.

סכבתי את הארגז לתוך החדר, יותר קרוב לאור, והסתרלתי בו. הוא היה מלא תזכורות, "לֵיזֶר-דִיסְקִים" עתיקים. ותמונות עשנות דו-ממדיות שקראו להם פעם "פואוגרפיות." גם-כן משיתי ממנו ילקוט ישן, ובו מצאתי צרור של דפים צהובים. שתי פותוגרפיות היו קשורות לצרור. איש ואישה הופיעו בהן. באחת מהן הם עמדו לפני איזה בנין פשוט, ובשניה, באמצע רחוב כפרי.

רציתי להראות את צרור הדפים להורים שלי. התחלתי להשיב אתו לילקוט, ואז ראיתי שהיה עוד משהו בו. היתה עוד פותוגרפיה בתחתית הילקוט. הפותוגרפיה הזאת לא היתה כל כך ישנה כמו האחרת. היא באה מתקופה אחרת, ומקום אחר. הופיע בו מישהו, בערך בגיל שלי, על גשר...

Yesterday, in a forgotten corner of our kibbutz storeroom, next to a pile of dusty decorations from our one-hundredth Israel Independence Day celebration, I found a wooden box. I had been in the storeroom many times before, but until yesterday, I hadn't paid any attention to the box. At least it hadn't occurred to me to open it.

I dragged the box into the center of the room, closer to the light, and looked inside. It was full of momentos, antique laser disks and old-fashioned, two-dimensional pictures -- the kind they used to call "photographs." I also pulled out an old briefcase, in which I found a bundle of yellowed paper. Two old photos were tied to the bundle. A man and a woman appeared in both of them. In one of the pictures they stood before a very plain-looking building, and in the other they stood in the middle of a country road.

I wanted to show the papers to my parents, so I began stuffing them back into the briefcase, but as I did so, I noteced that it contained one more object. Another photograph lay at the bottom of the briefcase. It was not quite as old as the others, and came from a different time and place. The photograph was of someone about my age, standing on a bridge...

Glossary

bal tash'hit - literally, "not to destroy." Rabbinic sources forbid the wanton or pointless destruction of any living or usable thing. This area of *halachah* is traditionally associated with Deuteronomy 20:19-20.

codes - "encyclopedias" of Jewish law developed by rabbis in the Middle Ages, based on earlier sources.

d'rash - A *d'rash* is a creative interpretation of a biblical text. Because a d'rash often serves as the focal point for a sermon, sermons are sometimes referred to as *d'rashim.*

garma - an Aramaic term, used in rabbinic sources to indicate an unintentional, indirect effect of an action. For example, it may be a baseball player's intention to hit a home run, but it would be garma, if in the process of hitting a home run, the ball happened to also hit a spectator sitting in the bleachers.

halachah - the norms, standards and expectations for living a Jewish life. The *halachah* specifies how a Jew should act in any given situation. The historical development of *halachah* is recorded in sources such as Mishnah, Talmud, and the great *halachic* codes of the middle ages (e.g., Maimonides' Mishneh Torah and Yosef Karo's Shulhan Aruch).

hasagat g'vul - literally, "reaching a border." A wide variety of *halachot* having to do with protection from undue interference, unfair competition and intrusiveness are grouped under the category of "*hasagat g'vul.*"

hug ha-aretz - literally, "The circle around the Earth." The expression is found in the book of Isaiah, where it apparently refers to the outer margin of space that encircles the Earth and lays forever beyond the grasp of earthly creatures.

l'havdil - a Hebrew colloquial expression meaning: The comparison I am in the process of making should not be taken too literally. Though I am suggesting that there is some similarity between these two things, there also remains an essential difference between them.

midrashim - interpretations of Biblical passages which are typically based on a nuance, non-explicit implication, or apparent inconsistency in the passage. Midrashim often involve imaginative reconstructions of Biblical events.

Mishna - a compilation of Jewish law, edited by Rabbi Y'hudah HaNasi about 210 C.E.

parashah - one of the fifty-four sections into which the Torah has been divided for public reading in the synagogue each year.

pidyon ha-ben - literally, "redeeming the son." It is a *mitzvah* mentioned several times in the Torah to "redeem" the firstborn son of Jews who are not themselves *cohanim* or *l'vi'im* thirty days after birth. This is done by presenting the child to a *cohen* and then symbolically "regaining" the child in exchange for a small amount of money. This *mitsvah* has been interpreted in several different ways. Rashi suggested that we redeem our first born because in ancient Canaan first born sons typically served as "*cohanim*" in each extended family. Since the Torah gave this task to the descendants of Aaron, we symbolically express our gratitude to them for freeing our firstborn from priestly responsibilities through *pidyon ha-ben*. The practice may also be associated with the death of the Egyptians' firstborn, prior to the Exodus from Egypt. According to this interpretation, we redeem our firstborn as an expression of gratitude for the protection afforded the firstborn Israelites when the Egyptian firstborn were struck down.

responsa - see **sh'aylot u-teshuvot**.

sh'aylot u-teshuvot - literally "questions and answers"; also known by the Latin term "responsa." Questions posed to Jewish scholars for a legal decision or clarification of the *halachah* are called "*sh'aylot*." Responses to such questions are called "*teshuvot*."

Tanach - the "Hebrew" or "Jewish Bible." The word *Tanach* is an acronym for Torah (the "Five Books of Moses"), *N'vi'im* (the twenty-one books of the prophets), and *K'tuvim* (the thirteen additional sacred writings).

Talmud - a compilation of Jewish law based on the Mishna. Parallel versions of the Talmud were codified in Palestine and Babylonia up through the fifth century C.E.

tsa'ar ba'alei ḥayim - literally, "pain to a living thing." Rabbinic sources forbid the causing of unnecessary pain to any living creature. This area of *halachah* is traditionally associated with several biblical texts, including Gen. 9:4 (which traditionally has been interpreted as forbidding the eating of a limb taken from a live animal) and Exodus 23:5 (and Deut. 22:4), which require that one assist in the freeing of a pack animal that has collapsed under its burden.

Selected Readings on Ecology and the Jewish Tradition

Ellen Bernstein and Dan Fink, *Let the Earth Teach You Torah* [Shomrei Adamah, Wyncote, Pennsylvania, 1992]

A Hadassah Study Guide, *Judaism and Ecology* [Hadassah and Shomrei Adamah, New York, 1993]

Elizabeth Roberts and Elias Amidon, *Earth Prayers From Around the World* [Harper Collins, San Francisco, 1991]

Aubrey Rose, *Judaism and Ecology* [Cassell, London and New York, 1992]

David Stein, ed., *A Garden of Choice Fruit: 200 Classic Jewish Quotes on Human Beings and the Environment* [Shomrei Adamah, Wyncote, Pennsylvania, 1991]

Rabbi Meir Zeichel, *Environmental Quality in the Jewish Sources* [in Hebrew, edited for the Office of Environmental Protection, Interior Department, State of Israel, Jerusalem, 5750 (1990)]

The Melton Journal, Spring 1991 and Spring 1992. Two issues devoted to Judaism and Ecology.